UNLOCK

LISTENING & SPEAKING SKILLS

4

Jeremy Day

CAMBRIDGE
UNIVERSITY PRESS

CAMBRIDGE
UNIVERSITY PRESS

University Printing House, Cambridge CB2 8BS, United Kingdom

Cambridge University Press is part of the University of Cambridge.

It furthers the University's mission by disseminating knowledge in the pursuit of education, learning and research at the highest international levels of excellence.

www.cambridge.org
Information on this title: www.cambridge.org/9781107650527

First published 2014

Printed in the United Kingdom by Latimer Trend

A catalogue record for this publication is available from the British Library

ISBN 978-1-107-63461-9 Listening and Speaking 4 Student's Book with Online Workbook
ISBN 978-1-107-65052-7 Listening and Speaking 4 Teacher's Book with DVD
ISBN 978-1-107-61525-0 Reading and Writing 4 Student's Book with Online Workbook
ISBN 978-1-107-61409-3 Reading and Writing 4 Teacher's Book with DVD

Additional resources for this publication at www.cambridge.org/unlock

CONTENTS

UNL⌀CK UNIT STRUCTURE

The units in *Unlock Listening and Speaking Skills* are carefully scaffolded so that students build the skills and language they need throughout the unit in order to produce a successful Speaking task.

UNLOCK YOUR KNOWLEDGE	Encourages discussion around the theme of the unit with inspiration from interesting questions and striking visuals.

WATCH AND LISTEN	Features an engaging and motivating *Discovery Education™* video which generates interest in the topic.

LISTENING 1	Provides information about the topic and practises pre-listening, while listening and post-listening skills. This section also includes a focus on a pronunciation feature which will further enhance listening comprehension.

LANGUAGE DEVELOPMENT	Practises the vocabulary and grammar from Listening 1 and pre-teaches the vocabulary and grammar from Listening 2.

LISTENING 2	Provides a different angle on the topic and serves as a model for the speaking task.

CRITICAL THINKING	Contains brainstorming, categorising, evaluative and analytical tasks as preparation for the speaking task.

PREPARATION FOR SPEAKING / SPEAKING SKILLS	Presents and practises functional language, pronunciation and speaking strategies for the speaking task.

SPEAKING TASK	Uses the skills and strategies learnt over the course of the unit to produce a presentational or interactional speaking task.

OBJECTIVES REVIEW	Allows learners to assess how well they have mastered the skills covered in the unit.

WORDLIST	Includes the key vocabulary from the unit.

This is the unit's main learning objective. It gives learners the opportunity to use all the language and skills they have learnt in the unit.

UNLOCK MOTIVATION

UNLOCK YOUR KNOWLEDGE

Work with a partner. Discuss the questions below.

1 What is deforestation?
2 What are the causes and consequences of it?
3 What other things do people do that affect the environment?
4 How can people use natural resources without destroying the environment?

PERSONALIZE

Unlock encourages students to bring their own knowledge, experiences and opinions to the topics. This **motivates** students to relate the topics to their own contexts.

DISCOVERY EDUCATION™ VIDEO

Thought-provoking videos from *Discovery Education™* are included in every unit throughout the course to introduce topics, promote discussion and motivate learners. The videos provide a new angle on a wide range of academic subjects.

" The video was excellent! It helped with raising students' interest in the topic. It was well-structured and the language level was appropriate.

Maria Agata Szczerbik,
United Arab Emirates University,
Al-Ain, UAE "

UNLOCK CRITICAL THINKING

" […] with different styles of visual aids such as ideas maps, grids, tables and pictures, this [Critical thinking] section [provides] very crucial tools that can encourage learners to develop their speaking skills.

Dr. Panidnad Chulerk, Rangit University, Thailand "

BLOOM'S TAXONOMY

CREATE — create, invent, plan, compose, construct, design, imagine

decide, rate, choose, recommend, justify, assess, prioritize — EVALUATE

ANALYZE — explain, contrast, examine, identify, investigate, categorize

show, complete, use, classify, examine, illustrate, solve — APPLY

UNDERSTAND — compare, discuss, restate, predict, translate, outline

name, describe, relate, find, list, write, tell — REMEMBER

BLOOM'S TAXONOMY

The Critical thinking sections in *Unlock* are based on Benjamin Bloom's classification of learning objectives. This ensures learners develop their **lower-** and **higher-order thinking skills**, ranging from demonstrating **knowledge** and **understanding** to in-depth **evaluation**.
The margin headings in the Critical thinking sections highlight the exercises which develop Bloom's concepts.

LEARN TO THINK

Learners engage in **evaluative** and **analytical tasks** that are designed to ensure they do all of the thinking and information-gathering required for the end-of-unit speaking task.

CRITICAL THINKING

At the end of this unit you are going to do the speaking task below.

How can we ensure that workers in developing countries are paid fairly for the food we import?

Understanding a pie chart
Pie charts are used to show percentages. The sections of a pie chart represent portions of 100%, or the entire circle.

UNDERSTAND

1 Look at the pie chart below. Answer the questions.

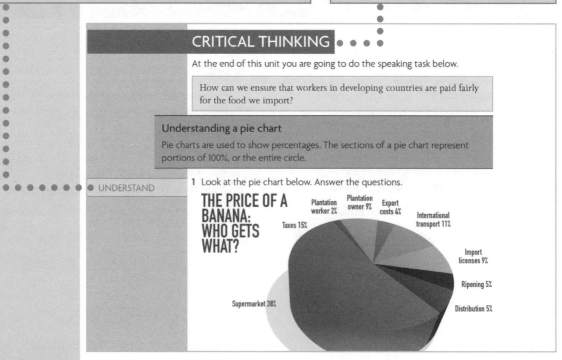

THE PRICE OF A BANANA: WHO GETS WHAT?

Plantation worker 2%
Plantation owner 9%
Export costs 4%
Taxes 15%
International transport 11%
Import licenses 9%
Ripening 5%
Distribution 5%
Supermarket 38%

UNL⌀CK RESEARCH

THE CAMBRIDGE LEARNER CORPUS ⊙

The **Cambridge Learner Corpus** is a bank of official Cambridge English exam papers. Our exclusive access means we can use the corpus to carry out unique research and identify the most common errors that learners make. That information is used to ensure the *Unlock* syllabus teaches the most **relevant language**.

THE WORDS YOU NEED

Language Development sections provide vocabulary and grammar-building tasks that are further practised in the UNL⌀CK ONLINE Workbook. The glossary provides definitions and pronunciation, and the end-of-unit wordlists provide useful summaries of key vocabulary.

⊙ LANGUAGE DEVELOPMENT

EXPLANATION

Verbs followed by *to* + infinitive

Some verbs are usually followed by *to* + infinitive. Common examples are *agree, arrange, consent, manage, offer, refuse, threaten* and *want*.

> We live close to both our daughters and **offer to babysit** our grandchildren regularly.

After certain verbs in active sentences an object is included an object before *to* + infinitive.

> Our savings allow us to live the life we've always wanted.

Ot
pe

1 Co

1

2

3

PRONUNCIATION FOR LISTENING

Listening for certain and uncertain intonation

We can sometimes understand a speaker's attitude by listening to their intonation. A rising intonation can indicate uncertainty and a falling intonation can indicate certainty about what they are saying.

6 🔊 2.2 Listen and write certain (C) or uncertain (U) next to the statements below.

1 You're considering university, aren't you?	U
2 I like maths and physics, and I'm doing well in those classes.	C
3 You should make use of your maths and physics abilities.	___
4 I'm considering studying engineering.	___

ACADEMIC LANGUAGE

Unique research using the **Cambridge English Corpus** has been carried out into academic language, in order to provide learners with relevant, academic vocabulary from the start (CEFR A1 and above). This addresses a gap in current academic vocabulary mapping and ensures learners are presented with carefully selected words which they will find essential during their studies.

PRONUNCIATION FOR LISTENING

This unique feature of *Unlock* focuses on aspects of pronunciation which may inhibit listening comprehension. This means that learners are primed to understand detail and nuance while listening.

❝ *The language development is clear and the strong lexical focus is positive as learners feel they make more progress when they learn more vocabulary.*
Colleen Wackrow,
Princess Nourah Bint Abdulrahman University, Al-Riyadh, Kingdom of Saudi Arabia ❞

UNL⊘CK SOLUTIONS

FLEXIBLE

Unlock is available in a range of print and digital components, so teachers can mix and match according to their requirements.

UNL⊘CK ONLINE WORKBOOKS

The **UNL⊘CK ONLINE** Workbooks are accessed via activation codes packaged with the Student's Books. These **easy-to-use** workbooks provide interactive exercises, games, tasks, and further practice of the language and skills from the Student's Books in the Cambridge LMS, an engaging and modern learning environment.

CAMBRIDGE LEARNING MANAGEMENT SYSTEM (LMS)

The Cambridge LMS provides teachers with the ability to track learner progress and save valuable time thanks to automated marking functionality. Blogs, forums and other tools are also available to facilitate communication between students and teachers.

UNL⊘CK EBOOKS

The *Unlock* Student's Books and Teacher's Books are also available as interactive eBooks. With answers and *Discovery Education™* videos embedded, the eBooks provide a great alternative to the printed materials.

UNL⦵CK TEACHING TIPS

1 Using video in the classroom

The *Watch and listen* sections in *Unlock* are based on documentary-style videos from *Discovery Education*™. Each one provides a fresh angle on the unit topic and a stimulating lead-in to the unit.

There are many different ways of using the video in class. For example, you could ask learners to listen to the audio track of the video without viewing the images and ask learners what the video is about. Then show the whole video and check whether the learners were correct. You could ask learners to reconstruct the voiceover or record their own commentary to the video. Try not to interrupt the first viewing of a new video, you can go back and watch sections again or explain things for struggling learners. You can also watch with the subtitles turned on when the learners have done all the listening comprehension work required of them. For less-controlled listening practice, use the video for free note-taking and ask learners to compare their notes to the video script.

See also: Goldstein, B. and Driver, P. (2014) *Language Learning with Digital Video*, Cambridge University Press, and the *Unlock* website www.cambridge.org/unlock for more ideas on using video in the classroom.

2 Teaching listening skills

Learners who aim to study at university will need to be comfortable listening to long, complex listening texts in a number of different genres. The listening texts in *Unlock Listening & Speaking Skills* provide learners with practice in the different listening sub-skills and also provide topic-related ideas and functional language needed for the *Speaking task*. Every unit focuses on one key listening skill, which is highlighted in a box, as well as various sub-skills, so that learners build on their listening skills throughout.

Before listening for the first time, use the *Preparing to listen* skills boxes to draw on learners' background knowledge and expectations of the listening text. Use the *While listening* skills boxes to focus students on listening sub-skills. Use the *Pronunciation for listening* activities to raise awareness of pronunciation features which can help listeners

decode speech. Learners have an opportunity for reflection on what they have listened to in the *Discussion* activities.

3 Teaching pronunciation

Unlock features *Pronunciation for listening* and *Pronunciation for speaking* sections. In *Pronunciation for listening*, learners focus on aspects of pronunciation which can enhance their listening comprehension, such as linking words, intonation, strong and weak forms in connected speech, homophones, etc. This will help learners to obtain more meaning from the listening text and in real life. Encourage learners to try using these pronunciation features in their own speaking so that they will be primed to hear them.

In *Pronunciation for speaking*, learners focus on aspects of pronunciation which they can put into practice in the *Speaking task*, such as consonant clusters, vowel sounds, connected speech, sentence stress and using intonation and tone. Practise pronunciation with your learners by recording them and giving feedback on the clarity, pace and stress in the *Speaking task*. Encourage your learners to record themselves and reflect on their own pronunciation.

4 Teaching speaking skills

Learners work towards the *Speaking task* throughout the unit by learning vocabulary and grammar relevant for the task, and then by listening to the key issues involved in the topic. Learners gather, organize and evaluate this information in the *Critical thinking* section and use it to prepare the *Speaking task*. *Unlock* includes two types of *Speaking task* – presentational and interactional. In the presentational tasks, learners will be required to give a presentation or monologue about the topic, often as part of a team. The interactional tasks require learners to role-play or interact with another person or persons.

There is an *Additional speaking task* for every unit in the Teacher's Book. This can be used as extra speaking practice to be prepared at home and done in class or as part of an end-of-unit test/evaluation. The *Additional speaking task* is also available on the Online Workbook. See section 8 for more details.

If your learners require IELTS test practice, point out that the discussion questions in the *Unlock your knowledge* sections provide practice of *IELTS Part 1 and 3* and the *Speaking tasks* provide practice of *IELTS Part 2*. Set the *Speaking task* as a timed test with a minimum time of two minutes and grade the learners on their overall fluency, vocabulary and grammar and the quality and clarity of their pronunciation.

5 Managing discussions in the classroom

There are opportunities for free discussion throughout *Unlock Listening & Speaking Skills*. The photographs and the *Unlock your knowledge* boxes on the first page of each unit provide the first discussion opportunity. Learners could be asked to guess what is happening in the photographs or predict what is going to happen or they could investigate the questions for homework in preparation for the lesson.

Throughout the rest of the unit, the heading *Discussion* indicates a set of questions which can be an opportunity for free speaking practice. Learners can use these questions to develop their ideas about the topic and gain confidence in the arguments they will put forward in the *Speaking task*.

To maximize speaking practice, learners could complete the discussion sections in pairs. Monitor each pair to check they can find enough to say and help where necessary. Encourage learners to minimize their use of L1 (their first language) and make notes for any error correction and feedback after the learners have finished speaking.

An alternative approach might be to ask learners to role-play discussions in the character of one of the people in the unit. This may free the learners from the responsibility to provide the correct answer and allow them to see an argument from another perspective.

Task checklists

Encourage your learners to reflect on their performance in the *Speaking task* by referring to the Task checklist at the end of the unit. The checklists can also be used by learners to reflect on each other's performance, if you feel that your learners will be comfortable doing so.

Additional speaking tasks

There are ten Additional speaking tasks in the Teacher's Book, one for each unit. These provide another opportunity to practise the skills and language learnt in the unit.

Model language

Model language in the form of functional expressions and conversation gambits follow the *Additional speaking tasks* to help learners develop confidence in their speaking ability by providing chunks of language they can use during the *Speaking task*. Photocopy the *Model language* and hand this to your learners when they plan and perform their writing task. Make sure learners practise saying them before they begin their task.

6 Teaching vocabulary

The *Wordlist* at the end of each unit includes topic vocabulary and academic vocabulary. There are many ways that you can work with the vocabulary. During the early units, encourage the learners to learn the new words by setting regular review tests. You could ask the learners to choose, e.g. five words from the unit vocabulary to learn. Encourage your learners to keep a vocabulary notebook and use new words as much as possible in their speaking.

7 Using the Research projects with your class

There is an opportunity for students to investigate and explore the unit topic further in the *Research projects* which feature at the end of each unit in the Teacher's Books. These are optional activities which will allow your learners to work in groups (or individually) to discover more about a particular aspect of the topic, carry out a problem-solving activity or engage in a task which takes their learning outside the classroom.

Learners can make use of the Cambridge LMS tools to share their work with the teacher or with the class as a whole. See section 8 for more ideas.

8 Using UNLOCK digital components: Online Workbook and the Cambridge Learning Management System (LMS)

The Online Workbook provides:

- additional practice of the key skills and language covered in the Student's Book through interactive exercises. The **UNLOCK ONLINE** symbol next to a section or activity in the Student's Book means that there is additional practice of that language or skill in the Online Workbook. These exercises are ideal as homework.

- *Additional speaking tasks* from the Teacher's Books. You can ask your learners to carry out the *Additional speaking tasks* in the

Online Workbook for homework. Learners can record their response to the task and upload the file for the teacher.

- a gradebook which allows you to track your learners' progress throughout the course. This can help structure a one-to-one review with the learner or be used as a record of learning. You can also use this to help you decide what to review in class.
- games for vocabulary and language practice which are not scored in the gradebook.

The Cambridge LMS provides the following tools:

- **Blogs**

The class blog can be used for free writing practice to consolidate learning and share ideas. For example, you could ask each learner to post a description of their holiday (or another event linked to a topic covered in class). You could ask them to read and comment on two other learners' posts.

- **Forums**

The forums can be used for discussions. You could post a discussion question and encourage learners to post their thoughts on the question for homework.

- **Wikis**

In each class there is a Wiki. You can set up pages within this. The wikis are ideal for whole-class project work. You can use the wiki to practise process writing and to train the students to redraft and proofread. Try not to correct students online. Take note of common errors and use these to create a fun activity to review the language in class.

See www.cambridge.org/unlock for more ideas on using these tools with your class.

How to access the Cambridge LMS and setup classes

Go to www.cambridge.org/unlock for more information for teachers on accessing and using the Cambridge LMS and Online Workbooks.

---

9 Using Unlock interactive eBooks

Unlock Listening & Speaking Skills Student's Books are available as fully interactive eBooks. The content of the printed Student's Book and the Student's eBook is the same. However, there will be a number of differences in the way some content appears.

If you are using the interactive eBooks on tablet devices in the classroom, you may want to consider how this affects your class structure. For example, your learners will be able to independently access the video and audio content via the eBook. This means learners could do video activities at home and class time could be optimized on discussion activities and other productive tasks. Learners can compare their responses to the answer key in their eBooks which means the teacher may need to spend less time on checking answers with the whole class, leaving more time to monitor learner progress and help individual learners.

10 Using mobile technology in the language learning classroom

By Michael Pazinas, Curriculum and assessment coordinator for the Foundation Program at the United Arab Emirates University.

The presiding learning paradigm for mobile technology in the language classroom should be to create as many meaningful learning opportunities as possible for its users. What should be at the core of this thinking is that while modern mobile technology can be a 21st century 'super-toolbox', it should be there to support a larger learning strategy. Physical and virtual learning spaces, content and pedagogy all need to be factored in before deciding on delivery and ultimately the technological tools needed.

It is with these factors in mind that the research projects featured in this Teacher's Book aim to add elements of hands-on enquiry, collaboration, critical thinking and analysis. They have real challenges, which learners have to research and find solutions for. In an ideal world, they can become tangible, important solutions. While they are designed with groups in mind, there is nothing to stop them being used with individuals. They can be fully enriching experiences, used as starting points or simply ideas to be adapted and streamlined. When used in these ways, learner devices can become research libraries, film, art and music studios, podcast stations, marketing offices and blog creation tools.

Michael has first-hand experience of developing materials for the paperless classroom. He is the author of the Research projects *which feature in the Teacher's Books.*

1 GLOBALIZATION

Learning objectives

👥👥👥 Go through the learning objectives with the class to make sure everyone understands what they can expect to achieve in this unit. Point out that students will have a chance to review these objectives again at the end of the unit.

Lead-in

👥👥👥 Students work in small groups to think of a country starting with each letter of the alphabet, plus the nationality adjective for each country. The first team to find at least 20 countries and nationality adjectives beginning with different letters is the winner. Note that there are no countries beginning with the letter *X* or *W*, and only one beginning with *O* (Oman), *Q* (Qatar) and *Y* (Yemen).

As a follow-up, when you are checking the lists of countries, elicit which part of the world they are in (e.g. the Middle East, Central America, North Africa, etc.).

UNLOCK YOUR KNOWLEDGE

👥 Students discuss the questions in pairs. Encourage them to think of answers from as many parts of the world as possible. After a few minutes, open up the discussion to include the whole class. Again, try to elicit examples from around the world, not just a few countries.

| Answers will vary.

WATCH AND LISTEN

Video script

THE GLOBALIZATION OF FOOD

▶ International trade is the activity of buying, selling and exchanging goods and services between countries. In the twenty-first century, industrialization, modern transportation, multinational corporations and outsourcing are all having a major impact on the international trade system.

Increasing international trade powers the continued growth of globalization. Food is one commodity that is traded worldwide. In Longsheng, China, rice farmers have worked in these rice paddies for almost 800 years. The rice they grow feeds people all over the world.

Countries trade produce with each other to sell what they grow in excess and they buy commodities that are cheaper elsewhere, or that they cannot produce themselves. France, for example, is only the 43rd

largest country in the world, but it is the world's second largest exporter of agricultural products, selling wheat, dairy and meat products to countries worldwide.

Competition is fierce between countries to gain a competitive advantage in the international trade market and to get a good price for their produce. In Australia, goods are transported far across the country by road and worldwide by ship. Australian farmers export around 60% of what they produce, earning the country more than 30 billion Australian dollars per year. The transport involved in international trade can, however, have massive effects on pollution and the environment.

International trade can also make countries more economically reliant on non-domestic trade for the production, processing and purchase of goods. These Mexican prickly pear farmers rely on selling their product in specialist food shops across the world. However, this export business has brought money – and hope – to an entire community, by creating jobs.

Without international trade, nations would be limited to the goods and services within their own borders. So, the food produced here wouldn't end up on a plate here.

PREPARING TO WATCH

UNDERSTANDING KEY VOCABULARY

1 👤👥👥 Go through the instructions with the class. Point out that they may need to change some of the words (e.g. make nouns singular or use the infinitive form of verbs) to match them to the definitions. Students then work alone to complete the exercise. They check in pairs and feed back to the class.

| Answers
| 1 e 2 b 3 a 4 f 5 d 6 g 7 c 8 h

Language note

Note the changes in stress in the following words: *to produce* (verb) → *produce* (noun); *to export* (verb) → *an export* (noun). Other words from this unit with the same pattern include: *import* (verb) / *import* (noun); *impact* (verb) / *impact* (noun); *transport* (verb) / *transport* (noun).

2 👥 Check that everyone understands the questions (especially the meaning of *fresh foods*, *locally* and *imported/import*). Students discuss the question in pairs. After a few minutes, open up the discussion to include the whole class. You may need to supply the names of some foods in English if students don't know any.

| Answers will vary.

Language note

Fresh foods are those which are not preserved (by canning, freezing, etc.), and which therefore need to be consumed soon after production.

WHILE WATCHING
UNDERSTANDING MAIN IDEAS

3 ▶ 👤👥 Go through the question with the class, making sure everyone understands that they are looking for the best description of the video topic, not just things that are mentioned in the questions. You may also need to check they understand the words *pollution*, *destroy* and *livelihood*. (See Language note below.) Play the video for students to choose the correct answer. They check in pairs and feed back to the class.

| **Answers**
Sentence 2 best describes the topic of the video.

Language note

A person's *livelihood* is their ability to earn a living, i.e. make enough money to support themselves.

A *prickly pear* is the fruit of a type of cactus, also known as *fig opuntia*.

For explanations of more vocabulary from this video, see the Optional activity after Exercise 4.

LISTENING FOR KEY INFORMATION

4 ▶ 👤👥 Students read through the eight questions first to check that they understand all the words. (See Language note, above.) Play the video for students to make notes of the answers. They discuss their answers in pairs and watch again if necessary. Go through the answers with the class.

Answers

1 Industrialization, modern transport, globalization, multinational corporations and outsourcing
2 800 years
3 1
4 60%
5 30 billion Australian dollars per year.
6 In specialist food shops across the world.
7 It has brought money and hope by creating jobs.

DISCUSSION

5 👥 Students discuss the question in pairs. After a few minutes, open up the discussion to include the whole class.

| Answers will vary.

LISTENING 1

PREPARING TO LISTEN
Predicting content

👥 Tell students not to look at their books and elicit from the class why it can be useful to predict content before listening to it. Students then read the information in the box to compare it with their ideas.

USING YOUR KNOWLEDGE

1 👥👥 Go through the instructions carefully with the class. Check that they understand all the topic words, especially *shipping* (transporting goods, not necessarily by ship) and *dairy*. (See Optional activity, above.) In pairs or small groups they discuss which topics might be mentioned in the programme and what might be said about each of them. Discuss briefly with the class, but do not give any answers as students will be listening to the audio to check their ideas.

WHILE LISTENING
LISTENING FOR GIST

2 (◀ 1.1) 👤👥 Play the recording for students to check their predictions. They discuss their answers in pairs and feed back to the class.

Answers
Topics 1, 2, 6 and 7.

Language note

- An *aisle* /aɪl/ is a corridor between in a supermarket, with shelves on either side. There are also aisles in aeroplanes and churches, with seats on either side.
- If you are *watching your weight*, you are on a diet, or being careful about eating too much.
- A *supply chain* is the group of people and businesses between a producer and a final consumer. For example, the supply chain for bananas may include growers, exporters, transportation companies, importers, wholesalers and retailers.
- Your *carbon footprint* is a calculation of the amount of carbon dioxide emissions that you create through your lifestyle choices. For example, if you travel to work by bus, you have a lower carbon footprint than someone who drives a car to work.

LISTENING FOR DETAIL

3 ◀) 1.1 👤👥 Students read through the statements to check they understand them and to predict whether they are true or false. Play the recording for students to check their answers. They discuss briefly in pairs and feed back to the class.

> **Answers**
> 1 T 2 T 3 F 4 F 5 F 6 F

POST LISTENING

LISTENING FOR OPINION

4 👥 Students work in pairs to discuss the opinion behind the three statements and chose the ones they think best match the radio programme. After a few minutes, open up the discussion to include the whole class.

> **Answers**
> 1 a 2 b 3 a

PRONUNCIATION FOR LISTENING

Consonant clusters

5 ◀) 1.2 👤👥 Write some minimal pairs of words on the board (*go/grow, spell/sell, clothes/close, etc.*). Say one word from each pair and ask the students to identify the word you said. Students read the advice in the box. Play the recording. Students underline the correct answer individually and check their answers in pairs.

> 1 going 2 tea 3 find 4 sewed 5 timed 6 Flying 7 pass 8 cost

6 ◀) 1.3 👥 Ask students to look at the words in red in the notes and guess why each word is a mistake. Advise them to check the context of the word to find the correct answer. Play the recording. Students correct the words. They check in pairs and feed back to the class.

> support; three; First; sixth; climate; state; trap; growing, would; rain

DISCUSSION

7 👥 Students work in pairs or small groups to discuss the questions. After a few minutes, open up the discussion to include the whole class.

> Answers will vary.

⊙ LANGUAGE DEVELOPMENT

THE ACTIVE AND PASSIVE VOICE

👥👥 Tell students to close their books. Write the following sentences on the board:

The UK imports bananas from Thailand.

Bananas are imported from Thailand.

Elicit the difference between the two sentences (The first uses the active voice; the second is in the passive voice.) and how to form the passive (verb *be* + past participle). Elicit situations when one form might be better than the other. You could also elicit how we could mention who imports the bananas in Sentence 2 (i.e. using *by* to introduce the agent). Then tell students to read the information in the box to check their ideas.

Language note

Another important use of the passive not mentioned in the explanation box on Page 31 is to draw particular attention to the agent by moving it to the end of a sentence (e.g. *This meal was cooked by my son*).

1 👤👥 Students work alone to label the statements. They check in pairs and feed back to the class.

Answers

1 P 2 A 3 A 4 P 5 P

2 👤👥 Students work alone to rewrite the sentences. With weaker classes, you could ask them to underline the object in each sentence first and elicit whether the agent could be included in each case. They check their answers in pairs and feed back to the class.

Answers

1 Fruit is shipped long distances.
2 Spanish tomatoes are imported.
3 A lot of produce in Spain is sold for export.
4 UK greenhouses / Greenhouses in the UK must be heated.
5 More information should be given (in supermarkets) about where fruit comes from.

Optional activity

👥 Students work in pairs to find and underline more examples of the passive in the script from Listening 1 on page 201/202. Check answers with the class.

Suggested answers

- David, did you realize that all of this fruit is imported from overseas?
- They have to be imported.
- It is possible to grow fruits and vegetables from hot countries here, but they have to be grown in greenhouses, …
- If you look at these tomatoes, which were grown on a local farm, …
- That was flown about 18,800 kilometres.
- … a huge amount of pollution was produced to get this food to the shelves.
- When food travels, a lot of carbon dioxide pollution is produced …
- This lettuce may have been grown in the local area, but it could have been transported across the country to be put into this plastic packaging.
- … food grown around the country is transported to large factories to be packaged or processed.
- It's sometimes then transported back to the place it was grown in the first place.

GLOBALIZATION AND ENVIRONMENT VOCABULARY

3 👤👥 Students work alone to complete the text. They check in pairs and feed back to the class.

Answers

1 carbon footprint 2 transportation 3 carbon dioxide emissions 4 processing 5 climate change 6 environment 7 supply chain 8 purchasing 9 produce 10 imported

LISTENING 2

PREPARING TO LISTEN

USING YOUR KNOWLEDGE

1 👥👥👥 Students discuss the questions in pairs or small groups. After a few minutes, open up the discussion to include the whole class.

Answers will vary.

WHILE LISTENING

LISTENING FOR MAIN IDEAS

2 🔊1.4 👤👥 Play the recording for students to put the statements in order. They check in pairs and feed back to the class.

Answers

a 3 b 5 c 1 d 2 e 4

LISTENING FOR DETAIL

3 🔊1.4 👤👥 Students work in pairs to try to remember which words in the box belong with which statistics in the pie chart. Play the recording a second time for them to check. They check again in pairs and feed back to the class.

Answers

households: 29%; processing: 20%; agriculture: 15%; wholesale & retail: 14%; food service: 12%; packaging: 6%; transportation: 4%

POST LISTENING

4 👤👥 Check that everyone understands the meaning of the word cause. You could ask the question What are some causes of global warming? to check this. Students then work alone to underline the cause of the action in each sentence. They check in pairs and feed back to the class.

Answers

1 ...general changes in lifestyle ...
2 You can buy fresh fruit and vegetables from all over the world...
3 ...aeroplanes creating pollution that causes environmental problems...
4 Experts argue that foods that are the least damaging to the environment are usually the ones grown locally.
5 These greenhouses are heated.

5 👤👥 Students work alone to circle the language that indicates the cause of the action in each sentence. They check in pairs and feed back to the class.

Answers

1 Due to 2 As a result 3 … because of
4 Consequently 5 …and therefore

6 👤👥 Using the prompts, students complete the sentences with their own ideas. Monitor during the activity to offer support and give students help with grammar and vocabulary if necessary. Students compare their sentences in pairs and feed back to the class.

Possible answers:

1 Due to improvements in food processing techniques, food now stays fresher for longer.
2 Food travels to supermarkets by aeroplane. As a result, we can buy fruits and vegetables from other countries all year round.
3 Locally grown foods have a smaller carbon footprint. Consequently, they are better for the environment.
4 Producing food packaging uses a lot of energy, which therefore results in a bigger carbon footprint for the food packaging companies.

DISCUSSION

7 👥 Students work in pairs to describe a meal they enjoy and discuss the questions. After a few minutes, open up the discussion to include the whole class.

Answers will vary.

CRITICAL THINKING

👫👫 Go through the final speaking task with the class. Elicit why the task is described as a complex situation (Suggested answer: because there are no easy solutions to the situation outlined.) and why data might be useful in the

task. (Suggested answer: because it will enable you to focus on the most important aspects of the situation when writing about it.)

UNDERSTAND

Understanding a pie chart

👫👫 Students close their books. Elicit from the class what a pie chart is and how it works. Students then look at the information in the box to check their ideas.

1 👥 Students work in pairs to discuss the questions. After a few minutes, open up the discussion to include the whole class. Make sure everyone fully understands the meanings of the words in the pie chart, especially *plantation, ripening* and *distribution*.

Answers

1 The percentage of the price of a banana that goes to each party involved in its production and distribution.
2 9
3 The other percentages in the chart would increase in size.

UNDERSTANDING DATA IN A PIE CHART

2 👥 Students work in pairs to discuss the five questions. After a few minutes, open up the discussion to include the whole class.

Answers

1 The amount of money the supermarket takes, at 38%.
2 The amount of money that goes to the plantation worker, at 2%.
3 International transportation.
4 Ripening contributes 5% to the price of bananas.
5 Import licences contribute 9% to the pie chart.

ANALYZE

ANALYZING AND USING DATA IN A PIE CHART

3 👤 Check that everyone understands the meaning of *support* (agree with) and *contradict* (disagree with) in this context. Students work alone to complete the exercise. They check in pairs and then feed back to the class.

Answers

1 C 2 C 3 S 4 C 5 C 6 C

4 👥 Students work in pairs to discuss the questions. After a few minutes, open up the discussion to include the whole class.

> ### Possible answers
> 1 Because they make a big profit by increasing the price of the bananas once they are in stores.
> 2 Because they are cheap to grow in their country of origin.
> 3 Because they pay their workers very low wages.
> 4 The supermarket section of the pie chart would probably increase, as supermarkets would have to pay less tax so their profits would increase.
> 5 The price of bananas would probably increase, as supermarkets would want to make the same amount of profit on the bananas they sell.

SPEAKING

PREPARATION FOR SPEAKING

Presenting data
👥 Tell students to read the information in the box and the advice it provides. You may need to check that everyone understands the meaning of *fractions* (parts of whole numbers, such as ½, ¾ and ⅝) and *sequential language* (phrases for showing the order of elements in a sequence, such as *firstly, next, finally* etc.).

1, 2 🔊 1.5 👤👥 Students work alone to complete the introduction. They check answers in pairs. Play the recording for them to check their ideas before feeding back to the class. Point out that the gapped phrases will all be useful for students to use in their own presentations later.

> ### Answers
> 1 I'd like to talk about 2 a lot of discussion
> 3 Many people believe 4 others have pointed out
> 5 They say 6 would like to show 7 look at 8 consider

DESCRIBING A PIE CHART

3 👤👥 Students work alone to complete the sentences. They check in pairs and feed back to the class.

> ### Answers
> 1 The largest part; more than a quarter of
> 2 accounts for
> 3 each make up; a total of
> 4 Three parts are related to; they make up

DRAWING CONCLUSIONS FROM DATA

4 🔊 1.6 👥 Students work in pairs to predict the most logical order of the expressions. Play the recording for them to check their answers. They check in pairs and listen a second time if necessary before feeding back to the class.

> ### Answers
> a 3 b 1 c 5 d 7 e 6 f 2 g 4

> ### Optional activity
> 👥 Students work in pairs to re-tell this extract of the presentation using the phrases from Exercises 3 and 4. When they have finished, you could play the extract again for them to compare it with their versions. Afterwards, ask some volunteers to re-tell the extract for the class.

5 👤👥 Students work alone to match the sentence halves. They check in pairs and feed back. Again, point out that the phrases will all be useful for students' own presentations.

> ### Answers
> 1 e 2 a 3 d 4 c 5 b

SPEAKING TASK

👥 Point out that this is the same task that students prepared for in the Critical thinking section. Tell students to look at the Task checklist after Exercise 6, so that they know what is expected of them. Elicit from the class which exercises from the Speaking section in this unit contain useful language for presentations (Exercise 1 has useful language for setting the context in the introduction; Exercise 3 has useful language for describing data; Exercise 4 has useful language for sequencing information; Exercise 5 has useful language for drawing conclusions).

PREPARE

1 👥 Students work in pairs to choose one of the three statements, and discuss whether they agree or disagree with it. Note that even if they choose a statement and prepare together, they will still give individual presentations.

2, 3, 4 👥 Students work in their pairs to discuss the questions for their statement and to plan the order of their presentations. They write notes and a conclusion to help organize the presentation.

PRACTISE

5 👥 Students then work in their pairs to prepare and practise their presentations. Allow plenty of time for this preparation stage, and monitor carefully providing support if necessary. Students then take turns to practise giving their presentation to their partner.

6 👥👥 Divide the class into small groups of around four students. Split up the original pairs so that each member of a pair ends up in a different group. Students take turns to give their presentations to their groups. While listening to each other's presentations, they should be ready to give feedback on the content and the language and delivery of the presentation. After each presentation, they give each other feedback. Make sure they know to be positive and constructive in their feedback. Monitor carefully while students are speaking to make notes of the good and bad examples of language that you hear. Pay particular attention to the phrases and structures from this unit. Afterwards, give and elicit feedback on the language used during the presentations.

TASK CHECKLIST / OBJECTIVES REVIEW

👥 Students complete the checklist in pairs and then report back to the class. Where they feel they need extra practice, discuss with the class how they can get this. You can also feed back on how well they are able to do the things in the table, and where they need extra practice.

WORDLIST

👥 Students work in pairs to explain the words in the list to a partner. Afterwards, ask volunteers to explain each word to the class.

REVIEW TEST

See page 97 for the photocopiable Review test for this unit and Teaching tips, page 90 for ideas about when and how to administer the Review test.

ADDITIONAL SPEAKING TASK

See page 117 for an Additional speaking task related to this unit.

Give each student a photocopy of the model language and additional speaking task on page 117. Students work in groups to think about the most interesting features of the pie chart and possible reasons for the figures. They then work alone to plan their presentations. Make sure they know to use the model language to draw conclusions about the data. Finally, students work with a partner to deliver their presentations. Finish off by discussing as a class which data they found most interesting.

RESEARCH PROJECT

Make a presentation about food journeys

Divide the class into groups and ask each group to compile a list of their favourite foods. The groups research one of these foods, including where it comes from, its effect on health, how it is produced and how many miles it travels to get to their country. Students could use online tools to record and share their research.

The information could be used for group presentations. Alternatively, the class could collate their information, producing a world map showing 'food routes' for each of the foods they have researched, or a graph to show the distances the food has travelled. The data could form a starting point for thinking about the environmental or health impact of different foods.

2 EDUCATION

Learning objectives

👥 Go through the learning objectives with the class to make sure everyone understands what they can expect to achieve in this unit. Point out that students will have a chance to review these objectives again at the end of the unit.

Lead-in

👥👥 Write the following quotes about education on the board or find them on the internet and print them out. Students work in pairs to decide what each quote means and if they agree with the opinion in them. You may need to support them to make sure they understand some of the more difficult words and structures in the quotes. When they are ready, open up a class discussion on the quotes. You could have a class vote to decide on the best quote.

- "Live as if you were to die tomorrow. Learn as if you were to live forever." (Mahatma Gandhi, Indian Independence Leader)
- "I have never let my schooling interfere with my education." (Mark Twain, American author)
- "Education is the most powerful weapon which you can use to change the world." (Nelson Mandela, former President of South Africa)
- "When you know better you do better." (Maya Angelou, American author and poet)
- "Kids don't remember what you try to teach them. They remember what you are." (Jim Henson, American film and TV director and producer, creator of 'Sesame Street' and 'The Muppets')

UNLOCK YOUR KNOWLEDGE

👥👥 Go through the questions with the class. Make sure everyone understands all the words, especially *internship*. (See Background note.) Students discuss the questions in pairs or small groups. After a few minutes, open up the discussion to include the whole class.

❙ Answers will vary.

Background note

An *internship* is a period of work experience, typically for university or college students to learn about the world of work. They may be paid or unpaid, and tend to involve office work rather than physical or technical work, where *apprenticeships* are more usual. For new graduates or college-leavers, experience of an internship can be the most valuable part of their CV, which will help them find paid work.

WATCH AND LISTEN

Video script

ASTRONAUT TRAINING

▶ Clay Anderson wears a suit to work. A space suit!

Clay has been training for the past nine years to work on NASA's International Space Station. His training is very practical, but it also needs to be theoretical – he needs maths and physics to understand the science of space travel before he leaves Earth. Preparing for work in space is a huge challenge. In space, astronauts are weightless – they float freely in the air. How can you prepare for that?

Clay trains for this part of the mission in an aeroplane, but how does it work? The plane is flown in a series of arcs – taking a curved path up and then down again. This allows the student astronauts to be weightless for about 30 seconds at a time. 30 seconds is long enough to see what working whilst weightless feels like, but for proper training, Clay and the other trainees need hours of practice.

And for that, they come here. This training pool is 60 metres long, 30 metres wide and 12 metres deep. It holds more than 22 million litres of water and is the largest indoor pool in the world. The facility has 200 employees and more than 60 divers who help with astronaut training. Clay and his mission partner are lowered into the pool and their suits are checked for leaks.

For every hour Clay plans to work in space, he needs to practise for seven hours in the pool. The work area in the pool is an exact copy of the space station. This gives Clay very practical experience with the station and with the tools he needs. Clay practises every part of the job he will need to do in space. He will work long hours and so he needs to be physically strong to do the job. After seven hours in the training pool, Clay is clearly exhausted, but happy with the progress of his training.

Clay: Long day, lots to do, tired hands, but it was all good.

After his training, Clay will be ready for his six month space mission. When he goes to work on the International Space Station, he will hopefully have prepared enough to find time to enjoy the view.

PREPARING TO WATCH

UNDERSTANDING KEY VOCABULARY

1 👤👥 Elicit briefly from the class what *astronaut training* might involve. Students then work alone to match the words with the definitions. They check in pairs and feed back to the class. You could elicit from the class how each word might be connected with the topic of astronaut training.

Answers

1 g 2 d 3 h 4 a 5 c 6 e 7 f 8 b

Background note

There is an important technical distinction between *weight* and *mass*. The mass of an object (e.g. an astronaut) is fixed, and doesn't change according to whether that object is on the ground or in space. Weight, on the other hand, is calculated by multiplying an object's mass by the effect of gravity. An astronaut can therefore be literally *weightless* in space, where gravity has no effect. You can also appear weightless in a swimming pool, where your weight is balanced by your buoyancy. *Buoyancy* in water is the result of your body being less dense than the water around you. Both you and the water are pulled downwards by gravity, but the pull on the higher-density water is stronger, which means you float in it.

Technically, an *arc* is part of the circumference (edge) of a circle or a similar shape. In a non-technical sense, the word can be used to describe any curved line.

2 Students read the statements and decide whether the skills are practical or theoretical. Note that some of the skills may involve elements of both, so in these cases students will need to decide which is the more prominent of the two. They check in pairs and feed back to the class.

Answers

Practical: 1, 3, 4, 6, 7
Theoretical: 2, 5, 8

WHILE WATCHING

UNDERSTANDING MAIN IDEAS

3 Play the video for students to tick the skills that are mentioned. They check in pairs and feed back to the class.

Answers

Skills 2,3 and 4.

UNDERSTANDING DETAIL

4 Students work in pairs to discuss what they remember about the questions. They watch the video again to check. They discuss the answers again briefly in pairs before feeding back to the class.

Answers

1 9 years 2 30 seconds 3 60; 30; 12 4 More than 22 million litres 5 200 6 7 hours 7 7 hours
8 6 months

Optional activity

Tell students to look at the script on page 203 and underline useful or difficult words. Students then work in small teams to find the answers to these questions. The first team to find all the answers is the winner.

1 What noun describes something that is difficult but can be enjoyable? (*a challenge*)

2 What verb describes what ducks do on water? (*float*)

3 What adjective describes a shape that isn't straight? (*curved*)

4 What noun is a general name for a place with a particular function? (*a facility*)

5 What noun describes a person who works underwater? (*a diver*)

6 What verb describes moving something down gently and gradually? (*lower*)

7 What noun describes a hole in an object or a covering, through which contents such as liquid or gas may accidentally pass? (*a leak*)

DISCUSSION

5 Students discuss the questions in pairs. After a few minutes, open up the discussion to include the whole class.

Answers

Answers will vary.

LISTENING 1

PREPARING TO LISTEN

UNDERSTANDING KEY VOCABULARY

1 Students work alone to complete the definitions with the words in the box. They check in pairs and feed back to the class.

Answers

1 specialist 2 vocational 3 apprentice 4 acquire
5 understanding 6 academic 7 mechanical 8 careers
adviser

2 Students work alone to complete the sentences with words from Exercise 1. They compare answers in pairs and feed back to the class.

Answers

1 careers adviser 2 mechanical 3 apprentice
4 acquire 5 understanding 6 vocational 7 academic
8 specialist

3 Students work in pairs. They take turns to describe their studies and career using the words in Exercise 1. Monitor, offering help with language if necessary. After a few minutes ask some students to share their partner's descriptions with the class.

> Answers will vary.

Language note

A *plumber* is a person who installs and fixes water installations, typically in people's homes.

The adjective *aeronautical* comes from the noun *aeronautics*, which is the science of designing and operating aircraft (aeroplanes, rockets, balloons, etc.).

WHILE LISTENING

LISTENING FOR MAIN IDEAS

4 (🔊 2.1) 🧍👥👥 Tell students to predict the answers to the questions based on the vocabulary from Exercise 1. Then play the recording for them to check their ideas. They compare their answers in pairs and feed back to the class.

> **Answers**
>
> 1 Which university course to choose.
> 2 Engineering.
> 3 They decide she should talk to some engineers and visit an engineering company.

LISTENING FOR DETAIL

5 (🔊 2.1) 👥👥 Students work in pairs to try to remember which advice the careers adviser gave Bahar. Then play the recording for students to check their ideas. They compare their answers in pairs again and feed back to the class.

> **Answers**
>
> 1 T 2 F 3 T 4 F 5 F 6 T 7 F 8 T

PRONUNCIATION FOR LISTENING

Certain and uncertain tones

👥👥 Tell students to close their books. Write the following sentence on the board: *I'm considering studying engineering.* Read it aloud twice, once with certain intonation (*I'm considering studying ↘ engineering*), once with uncertain intonation (*I'm considering studying ↗ engineering*).

Elicit from the class any differences they heard. Students then work in pairs to practise reading the sentence with both types of intonation. Tell students to look at the information in the box to compare it with their ideas.

6 (🔊 2.2) 🧍👥👥 Go through the instructions with the class, then play the recording for students to complete the exercise. They compare their answers in pairs and feed back to the class.

> **Answers**
>
> 3 C 4 U 5 C 6 C 7 U 8 C

POST LISTENING

7 🧍👥👥 Students work alone to identify and write the word or phrase in bold into the correct category. They check in pairs and feed back to the class.

> **Answers**
>
> | certain | uncertain |
> |---|---|
> | definitely | wonder |
> | for sure | considering |
> | | not sure |

Optional activity

🧍 Tell students to underline the parts of each expression that they could use in other situations to express their opinions or question those of others. Check answers with the class.

> **Suggested answers**
>
> 1 <u>It would definitely be</u> a way to use your talents.
> 2 So I'd like to study something technical, <u>that's for sure</u>.
> 3 <u>I wonder if I should</u> try something more vocational.
> 4 You're considering university, <u>aren't you?</u>
> 5 <u>I'm not sure if</u> engineering is for me.

DISCUSSION

8 👥👥 👥👥👥 Students discuss the questions in pairs or small groups. Remind them to use the phrases for certain and uncertain opinions in their discussions. After a few minutes, open up the discussion to include the whole class.

> Answers will vary.

⊙ LANGUAGE DEVELOPMENT

PREFERENCES

Stating preferences with *would*

👥 Tell students to close their books. Write the following extracts from Listening 1 on the board:

I'd like to study something technical.

I'd rather make something than write about it.

Elicit from the class what the two extracts have in common. (They both use *would* to state a preference.) Elicit from the class other ways of using *would* to state a preference. Then tell students to look at the information in the box to compare it with their ideas. Elicit which grammatical structures can come after each phrase with *would*. (See Language note.)

> ### Language note
>
> *Would rather* can be followed by either:
> - a bare infinitive: *I'd rather (not) go.*
> - a subject + past tense verb: *I'd rather you went / you didn't go.*
>
> *Would like* and *would prefer* can be followed by either:
> - a *to*-infinitive: *I'd like / I wouldn't like to go.*
> - a subject + *to*-infinitive: *I'd like / I wouldn't like you to go.*
> - a noun: *I'd like / I wouldn't like a new job.*
> - *it* + *if* + subject + past tense verb: *I'd like / I wouldn't like it if I had a new job.*
>
> In all cases, the meaning is future, not past.

1 👤👥 Students work alone to match the sentence halves. They check in pairs and feed back to the class.

> ### Answers
> 1 e 2 b 3 f 4 d 5 c 6 a

2 👤👥 Students work alone or in pairs to rewrite the sentences. Encourage them to use a range of structures from the box and Exercise 1 in their answers. When they are ready, ask volunteers to share their ideas with the class.

> ### Possible answers
> 1 Would / Wouldn't you prefer to earn a lot of money?
> 2 I'd rather study a diploma course.
> 3 Would they like to apply for university in Riyadh?
> 4 He'd rather consider studying medicine.
> 5 Would / Wouldn't she like to do a theoretical course?
> 6 I'd rather not start working right away.

ACADEMIC ADJECTIVES TO DESCRIBE PROFESSIONS

3 👤👥 Check that everyone understands what a *profession* is. (A job, typically one that requires skill and training.) Students then work alone to match the words with the definitions. They check in pairs and feed back to the class.

> ### Answers
> 1 h 2 c 3 a 4 g 5 f 6 b 7 e 8 d

> ### Background note
>
> *Professional* has two meanings. One relates to whether a person is paid or not: a *professional footballer* is paid to play football; an *amateur footballer* plays for fun. The second meaning relates to so-called *professions*, such as law, medicine, education and engineering, which only people with certain qualifications can join. This second meaning is the one used in Exercises 3 and 4.

4 👤👥 Students work alone to complete the text. They check answers in pairs and feed back to the class.

> ### Answers
> 1 medical 2 technical 3 physical 4 manual
> 5 professional 6 complex 7 secure 8 nuclear

LISTENING 2

PREPARING TO LISTEN

UNDERSTANDING KEY VOCABULARY

1 👥 Tell students to close their books. Write the words *Emergency Medical Technician* (EMT) and *Emergency Room Nurse* (ERN) on the board. Elicit from the class what an *emergency* is and what the two jobs might involve. Tell students to read Adam's notes and compare them with their ideas. You may need to check they understand the words *assess*, *procedure*, *condition* and *self-confident*. Students then work in pairs to discuss the questions. Point out that these are predictions at this stage – they will find out the answers in Listening 2. Discuss their ideas briefly as a class, but avoid confirming or rejecting them, as this would undermine the next exercise.

> ### Answers
> Answers will vary. These are students' predictions at this stage.

WHILE LISTENING

LISTENING FOR GIST

2 (◀) 2.3 Play the recording for students to check their predictions. They compare their answers in pairs and feed back to the class.

Answers

An Emergency Room Nurse has to work more closely with hospital staff.
An EMT needs to make decisions on their own.
An EMT needs to be sure in their self and their abilities.
An Emergency Room Nurse needs more training.
An EMT job has more excitement and adventure.
Becoming an Emergency Room Nurse requires more study.

LISTENING FOR OPINION

UNDERSTANDING EXPRESSIONS OF OPINION

3 (◀) 2.3 Go through the instructions carefully to make sure everyone understands how to complete the table, using the answers in the first row as an example. Students work in pairs to remember which person expressed which opinion, and which job they were describing. Play the recording again for students to check their ideas. They compare their answers in pairs again and feed back to the class.

Answers

2		X	X	
3		X	X	
4		X		X
5		X	X	
6	X			X
7	X		X	
8		X	X	

POST LISTENING

4 Tell students to close their books. Elicit from the class how you might infer something from a speaker when you are listening. Then tell students to look at the information in the box to compare it with their ideas. Students discuss the questions in pairs. When they are ready, open up the answers to a class discussion. Make it clear that there are no right or wrong answers to the questions as long as students can justify the choices they have made.

Possible answers

1 The adviser probably thinks Adam should do the EMT course, as he is so enthusiastic about it.
2 Probably helping people, being independent and making decisions on his own. He speaks more and his tone is more positive when he talks about these factors of the EMT job.
3 Whether the adviser and Adam's intonation is rising or falling when they are discussing different aspects of the two jobs he is considering.

DISCUSSION

5 Make sure everyone understands the meaning of natural ability. (Something you can do without trying.) Students then discuss the questions in pairs or small groups. After a few minutes, open up the discussion to include the whole class.

Answers will vary.

CRITICAL THINKING

Go through the final speaking task with the class. You can also get students to predict what kind of scholarship might feature in the speaking task – this will be explained fully later.

Prioritizing criteria

Tell students to close their books. Elicit from the class what prioritizing criteria might involve and why it might be useful when making a difficult decision. Note that the word criteria is included in the Optional activity above. Students look at the information in the box to compare it with their ideas.

EVALUATE

1, 2 Check that everyone understands all the words in the criteria, especially challenged and secure. Students then work alone to put the criteria in order. When they are ready, they compare and discuss their answers in pairs. Ask volunteers from each pair to present their top five answers to the class.

Answers will vary.

Using priorities to evaluate opinions

👥 Tell students to read the information in the box. Elicit some examples of groups of people who might need to decide how to spend a fixed amount of money (e.g. a marketing team planning how to promote a new product). Also elicit some examples of other resources that people may need to plan how to use. (Time, people, machines, office space, etc.)

3, 4 👥 👥👥 Students work in pairs to read the information and then discuss the task. Point out that there is no correct answer to the exercise. Students then compare the prioritization of their criteria with another pair. After a few minutes, open up the discussion to include the whole class.

| Answers will vary.

Background note

The *Mah Scholarship* has been invented for this book, but is based on similar scholarships around the world.

APPLY

5, 6 👥 👥👥 Students read the profiles and discuss the questions in pairs. After a few minutes, put them with another pair to compare their answers. Ask some volunteers to report back their ideas to the class.

| Answers will vary.

SPEAKING

PREPARATION FOR SPEAKING

GIVING AN OPINION AND MAKING SUGGESTIONS

1, 2 🔊 2.4 👤 👥 Students work alone to match the sentence halves and decide if the sentences are opinions or suggestions. Play the recording for students to check their ideas. They compare their answers in pairs and feed back to the class.

Answers

1 e 2 d 3 a 4 f 5 c 6 b
1, 2 and 6 give an opinion. 3, 4 and 5 are suggestions.

Agreeing and disagreeing respectfully with a speaker

👥👥 Tell students to close their books. Write the heading *Agreeing and disagreeing respectfully with a speaker* on the board. Elicit from the class why it might be important to show respect while agreeing or disagreeing with someone, and some techniques for doing this. Then tell students to look at the information in the box to compare it with their ideas.

3 👤 👥 Students work alone to complete the exercise. They check in pairs and feed back to the class.

Answers

1 D 2 A 3 A 4 D 5 D 6 D 7 A 8 A

4 👥 Divide the class into pairs and assign roles A and B to the two students. If you have an odd number of students, make a group of three where each student takes two statements instead. Students then take turns to read their statements aloud. Their partner should respond respectfully, using the phrases from Exercise 3 and their own ideas.

| Answers will vary.

Optional activity

👥👥 You could turn the statements from Exercise 4 into a full class discussion, where everyone has a chance to express their real opinion on all six statements. Encourage them to use the language from Exercise 3 to do this.

COMPROMISING AND FINALIZING A DECISION

5, 6 👤 👥 🔊 2.5 Students work alone to complete the sentences. They compare their answers in pairs then listen and check. They compare in pairs again and feed back to the class.

Answers

1 understandable 2 point 3 right 4 that 5 decision
6 agreement

PRONUNCIATION FOR SPEAKING

7 👤 👥 🔊 2.5 Explain that students should draw arrows next to the statements in Exercise 5 to show rising (➚) or falling (➘) intonation. Play the recording again for students to mark the intonation. They compare their answers in pairs and feed back to the class.

Answers
Uncertain: 1, 3, 4
Certain: 2, 5, 6

8 Students work in pairs to practise saying the sentences with both types of intonation, and to guess their partner's intonation. Monitor carefully and offer support where necessary.

SPEAKING TASK

Point out that this is the same task that students prepared for in the Critical thinking section. Tell them to look at the Task checklist after Exercise 4, so that they know what language they are expected to use in the task. Elicit from the class which exercises from the Preparation for speaking section in this unit contain useful language for this type of discussion (Exercise 1 has useful language for giving an opinion and making suggestions; Exercise 3 has useful language for agreeing and respectfully disagreeing; Exercise 5 has useful language for compromising and finalizing a decision).

PREPARE/PRACTISE

1, 2, 3 Divide the class into groups of 4–6 students. Students then work through the tasks in their groups. Monitor carefully and provide support where necessary.

DISCUSS

4 Ask a volunteer from each group to present and justify their decisions. You could allow a short inter-group discussion to discuss any differences between their first choices. Monitor carefully while students are speaking to make notes of the good and bad examples of language that you hear. Pay particular attention to the phrases and structures from this unit. Afterwards, give and elicit feedback on the language used during the discussion.

TASK CHECKLIST / OBJECTIVES REVIEW

Students complete the checklists in pairs and then report back to the class. Where they feel they need extra practice, discuss with the class how they can get this. You can also feed back individually to them on how well they are able to do the things in the table, and where they need extra practice.

WORDLIST

Students work in pairs to explain the words in the list to a partner. Afterwards, ask volunteers to explain each word to the class.

REVIEW TEST

See page 99 for the photocopiable Review test for this unit and Teaching tips, page 90 for ideas about when and how to administer the Review test.

ADDITIONAL SPEAKING TASK

See page 118 for an Additional speaking task related to this unit.

Write the main question in the task on the board and brainstorm a list of possible courses with students, asking them to justify their suggestions briefly by saying why/how they might be useful. Give each student a photocopy of the model language and additional speaking task on page 118. Students work alone to assign and write down marks for the five courses, as this will make te later negotiation stages more effective. They then work in small groups to discuss their choices. Make sure each student gets a chance to present their preference and justify their choice, before they try to reach a group agreement. At the end of the exercise, you could open up the discussion to include the whole class.

RESEARCH PROJECT

Create a video about a course at university

In groups, ask the class to make a list of some of the courses on offer at universities in their country. Each group should then choose one to research, finding out how long the course is, the topic areas it covers, student opinions for studying it, and what type of careers the course can lead to. Students could find this information online or by contacting the university and/or students directly.

Each group then produces a five-minute video about the course for people considering studying that subject at university. Students will need to create a script, think about who in the group will film the video, who will edit it, and who will present the information. The videos could then be uploaded to a video-sharing website.

3 MEDICINE

Learning objectives

👥 Go through the learning objectives with the class to make sure everyone understands what they can expect to achieve in this unit. Point out that students will have a chance to review these objectives again at the end of the unit.

Lead-in

👥 Students work in teams to brainstorm medical vocabulary for the following categories. (You could add your own categories to make the exercise more challenging).

- Illnesses
- People involved in medicine
- Places involved in medicine
- Medical equipment
- Medical verbs
- Medical procedures (ways of helping sick people)

The first team to think of at least four words in each category, or 30 words in total, is the winner.

Possible answers

- Illnesses: *cold, flu, cancer, malaria, measles,* etc.
- People involved in medicine: *doctor, nurse, surgeon, patient, chemist/pharmacist,* etc.
- Places involved in medicine: *hospital, surgery, ward, operating theatre, chemist's/pharmacy,* etc.
- Medical equipment: *needle, stethoscope, bandage, scalpel, crutch, IV (intravenous) drip,* etc.
- Medical verbs: *treat/cure* (an illness), *operate* (on sb), *perform* (an operation), *undergo* (an operation), *recover* (from an illness), etc.
- Medical procedures: *tablet, injection, operation, surgery, rehabilitation,* etc.

UNLOCK YOUR KNOWLEDGE

👥 👥 Make sure everyone understands all the words in the questions, especially *spread* and *vaccine*. (See Background note.) Students discuss the question in pairs or small groups. After a few minutes, open up the discussion to include the whole class.

Background note

A ***vaccine*** /ˈvæksiːn/ is a medical preparation used to prevent diseases. It is made from biological agents which are similar to disease-causing agents. The patient's body creates *antibodies* (a type of protein which attacks bacteria and viruses) to fight the vaccine. The same antibodies then protect the patient from the disease in question.

❙ Answers will vary.

WATCH AND LISTEN

Video script

ANTHRAX

▶ In two thousand and six, a New York drummer and drum-maker, named Vado Diomande, became seriously ill. The doctors did tests to diagnose the problem and were shocked by the results. Vado had anthrax.

Anthrax is one of the world's most dangerous diseases. Whenever a case of anthrax is discovered, government authorities are notified immediately. Government scientists, doctors, and experts must protect the health and safety of the public.

Anthrax spores occur naturally, found in soil and in animal products. Animals can carry the disease without being ill, but humans can't. The spores are invisible, and if inhaled, humans can become extremely ill, very quickly. Inhaled anthrax spores replicate and produce chemicals that destroy the human body.

Anthrax can only spread through spores, so Vado couldn't infect other people. Anthrax is rare, but an outbreak could kill tens of thousands of people in just days. It is important to identify cases of anthrax quickly. Fortunately, the disease can be treated if it is identified early. The doctors had to act quickly. The disease was treated with antibiotics and special anthrax drugs.

The experts couldn't understand how Vado had contracted anthrax, and equally, whether other people were going to catch it. They searched Vado's home for clues and found a trace of anthrax in the apartment – but it wasn't the source. But when they checked Vado's drum-making workshop, they discovered the source of the disease: animal skins that had been used for making drums. The skins, with the anthrax, had come from Africa.

Fortunately, Vado's treatment worked and he made a full recovery.

PREPARING TO WATCH

UNDERSTANDING KEY VOCABULARY

1 👤👥 Tell students to close their books. Elicit from the class what they know or can guess about anthrax. (See Background note below.) Students then work alone to read the text and match the words with the definitions. They check in pairs and feed back to the class.

> ### Answers
> 1 b 2 g 3 j 4 a 5 h 6 d 7 i 8 c 9 e 10 f

Optional activity

👥 Students work in pairs to decide where the stress falls in each of the words in Exercise 1: the first or only syllable, the second syllable or the third or later syllable. Note that one word (*diagnose*) can be pronounced in two ways, with no difference in meaning. When you check with the class, the pair with the most correct answers is the winner.

> ### Answers
> First or only syllable: <u>spo</u>res, <u>out</u>break, <u>dia</u>gnose, <u>treat</u>
> Second syllable: dis<u>ease</u>, oc<u>curs</u>, con<u>tract</u>, in<u>haled</u>, re<u>co</u>very
> Third or later syllable: diag<u>nose</u>, antibi<u>o</u>tics

---

USING YOUR KNOWLEDGE TO PREDICT CONTENT

2 👥 Students discuss the questions in pairs. After a few minutes, open up the discussion to the whole class. Avoid confirming or rejecting their ideas as this will undermine the next exercise.

> Answers will vary.

Background note

- As the text explains, *anthrax* is extremely dangerous. Before the 20th century, it was responsible for the deaths of hundreds of thousands of people and animals. A successful anthrax vaccine was created by French scientist Louis Pasteur in 1881. It is now extremely rare, especially in richer countries.
- Note the meaning and pronunciation of the verb *contract* /kənˈtrækt/, which is very different from the noun *contract* /ˈkɒntrækt/ (a legally-binding agreement).
- A *spore* is a type of seed produced by a plant or fungus, which then grows into a new plant/fungus, as part of its reproductive cycle. Technically, the spores that carry anthrax are not true spores, but rather *endospores*, which are versions of bacteria. They can lie dormant (inactive) and survive for hundreds or even thousands of years.

WHILE WATCHING

UNDERSTANDING MAIN IDEAS

3 ▶👤👥 Students watch the video and decide if the sentences true or false. They discuss their answers in pairs and feed back to the class.

> ### Answers
> 1 T 2 F 3 F 4 F 5 T 6 T

LISTENING FOR KEY INFORMATION

4 ▶👥 Students work in pairs to try to remember the missing information. They then watch the video a second time to check their ideas and complete the notes. They check in pairs and feed back to the class.

> ### Answers
> 1 2006 2 drummer and drum-maker 3 government authorities 4 soil and animal products 5 the spores are inhaled 6 tens of thousands 7 antibiotics and special anthrax drugs 8 animal skins from Africa

DISCUSSION

5 👥👥👥 Students discuss the questions in pairs or small groups. After a few minutes, open up the discussion to include the whole class.

> Answers will vary.

LISTENING 1

PREPARING TO LISTEN

USING YOUR KNOWLEDGE

1, 2 👥 Elicit from the class what a *pandemic* might be. Students then look at the map to check their ideas and discuss the questions in pairs. When they are ready, discuss the answers with the class. Avoid confirming or rejecting their ideas at this stage, as this will undermine the next exercise.

Background note

- The name *pandemic* comes from Greek and is related to the word *epidemic*, which describes a situation when occurrences of a particular disease in a particular area are far more than expected. A *pandemic* is an epidemic over a wider geographical area.

- If a disease is *contagious*, it passes easily from one person to the next through direct physical contact. Not all diseases are contagious. Examples of non-contagious infectious diseases include those transmitted by mosquitoes, and those that spread by transfer of bodily fluids (e.g. blood) from one person to another.
- *The flu* is an abbreviation of *influenza*, a disease which causes symptoms which are similar to (but more severe than) common colds. The name flu is also used for the illness *stomach flu* (gastroenteritis), which is unrelated to influenza.
- *Cholera* /ˈkɒlərə/ is a bacterial infection caused by drinking dirty water. It causes diarrhoea and vomiting, which can lead to severe dehydration and, in many cases, death.

WHILE LISTENING

LISTENING FOR GIST

3 (�)) 3.1 👥👥 Play the recording for students to check their ideas for Exercises 1 and 2. They compare their answers in pairs and feed back to the class.

Answers

Countries at a high-risk of a pandemic have dense populations living in large cities, a lot of international airports and many borders with other countries. High-risk countries are represented by dark blue on the map, graduating to light blue countries, which are low-risk.

Background note

- *Measles* is a viral infection, best known for causing a red rash on the skin of its victims. It is highly contagious, and there is no known treatment, but it is generally not serious, mostly causing discomfort.
- *Malaria* is an infectious disease transmitted by mosquitoes. Hundreds of millions of people are infected with malaria every year, and although most of them recover, the disease still kills around a million people every year.

4, 5 (�)) 3.1 👥👥👤 Go through the instructions for the exercise carefully with the class and tell students to discuss the table in pairs to try to see if they can remember what was said about each idea in Exercise 3 before listening again. Suggest that students make brief notes in the table, rather than writing full sentences. Play the recording again for students to complete the chart. Students compare their answers in pairs and listen again if necessary. Go through the answers with the class.

Answers

idea for stopping the spread of disease	viewpoint 1	viewpoint 2
Governments must make sure populations are in good health and live in good conditions.	*There's a limit to what governments can do in times of economic difficulty.*	*Governments don't always have the power to say exactly how everyone should live.*
Everyone should be forced to take vaccines.	(1) A vaccine that worked well last year may not be effective this year.	(2) A lot of people don't want to have a vaccine that might not work.
People with diseases shouldn't be allowed into the country.	(3) People spread diseases before they know they have them.	(4) It would be impossible to set up a system for checking if people have a disease.
All flights from countries with a pandemic should be stopped.	(5) It would have a terrible effect on the economy.	(6) It would stop a lot of people going to work, and it could separate families.

POST LISTENING

6 👥👥 👥👥👥 Elicit from the class what question tags are and how they are formed. (See Language note below.) Prior to doing Exercise 6, ask students to identify the question tags in Sentences 1, 2 and 3 (*can they?*, *shouldn't we?* and *wouldn't it?*). Students discuss the questions in pairs. When they are ready, open up the answers to a class discussion. Make it clear that there are no right or wrong answers to the questions as long as students can justify the choices they have made.

Possible answers:

1 People shouldn't be given a vaccination if they don't believe it will work.
2 We should stop all flights out of our country when there is a pandemic.
3 We have to consider the effects on business of any rules made to stop people travelling if there is a pandemic.

Language note

Question tags have two functions:

- To turn a statement into a question, when you don't know the answer, e.g. *That's right, isn't it?*
- To encourage a response from the person you are talking to, even though you know the answer to your own question, e.g. *It's cold, isn't it?*
- The first function is marked by rising intonation, like all questions. The second type has falling intonation, like statements.

Question tags have two parts:

- The same auxiliary verb (e.g. *will, can, do, have, be*) as the sentence. If the sentence does not have an auxiliary verb, *do/does/did* is used in the question tag. Positive sentences usually have negative tags, and vice versa.
- A pronoun to represent the subject (e.g. *we, it, you*). The dummy-subject *there* can also be used (e.g. *There's a problem, isn't there?*)

PRONUNCIATION FOR LISTENING

Intonation in question tags

👥 Tell students to close their books. Write the sentence '*That's right, isn't it?*' on the board. Elicit (or, if necessary, model) the two ways of pronouncing the sentence – first as a statement and then as a question – and the difference in meaning between the two versions. Tell students to look at the information in the box to compare it with their ideas, or simply read it if they struggled with defining the two ways of pronouncing the sentence.

7 (◀) 3.2 👥👥 Go through the instructions with the class and play the first two sentences so that everyone has a chance to hear the difference between the two types of intonation. Play the full recording for students to complete the exercise. They compare their answers in pairs and feed back to the class.

Answers
3 Q 4 S 5 Q 6 S 7 S 8 S

8 👥 Students work in pairs to practise reading the sentences and guessing their partner's intonation. Monitor carefully and provide support where necessary.

Optional activity

Tell students to look at the beginning of the video script on page 205 (e.g. the first five or six sentences, depending on how much time you want to devote to practising question tags). They work in pairs to add question tags to each sentence, splitting longer sentences to make it easier to add question tags if appropriate. When they are ready, ask volunteers to report their statements back to the class, using either question or statement intonation. Note that real English obviously uses question tags much less frequently than in this light-hearted example.

Suggested answers

In 2006, a New York drummer and drum-maker, named Vado Diomande, became seriously ill, didn't he?
The doctors did tests to diagnose the problem, didn't they?
And they were shocked by the results, weren't they?
Vado had anthrax, didn't he?
Anthrax is one of the world's most dangerous diseases, isn't it?
Whenever a case is discovered, government authorities are notified immediately, aren't they?
Government scientists, doctors and experts must protect the health and safety of the public, mustn't they?

DISCUSSION

9 👥 👥👥 Students discuss the questions in pairs or small groups. Encourage them to use question tags in their discussion. After a few minutes, open up the discussion to include the whole class.

Answers will vary.

⊙ LANGUAGE DEVELOPMENT

CONNECTING ACTIONS

Connecting actions with time expressions

👥 Tell students to close their books. Write the words *before, after, until, between, during,* and *throughout* on the board. Elicit from the class what they mean, along with example sentences using the expressions. Then tell students to look at the information in the box to compare it with their ideas.

Language note

Like all prepositions, prepositions of time are followed by noun phrases. A few prepositions of time (*before*, *after*, *until*) can also be used as conjunctions, in which case they are followed by clauses (i.e. a subject and verb).

- She looked fine *before/after/until* her illness (preposition + noun phrase)
- She looked fine *before/after/until* she was ill (conjunction + clause)
- She looked terrible *during/throughout* her illness. (preposition + noun phrase)
- NOT: ~~She looked terrible during/throughout she was ill.~~

We use *as of* or *as from* to mark the beginning of a period of time in the future:

- *As of* next Tuesday (beginning point), you can contact me at my new address (situation over a period of time).

Until and *till* have the same meaning – *till* is less formal. We use them to describe the end-point of a period of time:

- I didn't feel well (for a period of time) *until* I took my medicine (end-point).
- I stayed in hospital (period of time) *until* I could walk again (end-point).

We use *throughout* for states and actions that happened constantly or repeatedly for a whole period of time:

- She was awake *throughout* the operation. (state)
- She visited me *throughout* my time in hospital. (repeated action)

Up to has a similar meaning to *until*, but is much less frequent. We usually use it with dates, ages, etc.

- *Up to* the age of 14, she had never been to hospital.

1 👤👥👥 Students work alone to underline parts of/ the whole sentences as relevant. They check in pairs and feed back to the class.

Answers

1 During the pandemic, many people died because they didn't receive a vaccine.
2 Flu vaccines have improved a lot since their invention in 1914.
3 Before we make a vaccine, we have to try to guess how the flu is going to change.
4 After the 1918 pandemic, doctors got to work trying to develop a flu vaccine.
5 They need to be able to get vaccines to the people from the moment an outbreak occurs.
6 Throughout a pandemic, people should be reminded to take precautions.
7 International travel should be stopped until the pandemic has been contained.

2 👤👥👥 Students work alone to complete the sentences. Encourage them to experiment with some of the less common expressions, rather than simply using words like *before* and *after*. They compare their answers in pairs and feed back to the class.

Suggested answers

1 After 2 during, throughout 3 Between 4 until, before 5 After 6 until 7 until, up to 8 After

SCIENTIFIC RESEARCH VOCABULARY

3 👤👥👥 Students work alone to match the words with the definitions. They check in pairs and feed back to the class. Make sure everyone knows how to pronounce all the words, especially *proven*/ˈpruːvən/, *trial* /traɪl/ and *data* /deɪtə/.

Answers

1 e 2 b 3 h 4 g 5 d 6 a 7 f 8 c

Language note

- *Proven* is the past participle of the verb *to prove*. Some people use a regular participle (e.g. *They have proved/proven their theory*) when it is used in the perfect tense, but *proven* must be used when it is used as an adjective (e.g. *It's a ~~proved~~/proven fact*).

4 👤👥👥 Students work alone to complete the text. They check in pairs and feed back to the class.

Answers

1 proven 2 scientific 3 researchers 4 controlled 5 precautions 6 data 7 clinical 8 trials

LISTENING 2

PREPARING TO LISTEN

USING YOUR KNOWLEDGE

1 👥👥👥 Check that everyone understands what the *flu* is. (See Background note in Listening 1, above.) Students work in pairs to predict the answers to 1–4. Make sure they actually circle their predictions (not just the correct answers from Exercise 2), as these predictions will be useful for Exercise 4. After a few minutes, open up the discussion to include the whole class. Avoid confirming or rejecting their ideas as this will undermine the next exercise.

2 (� 3.3) 👤👥 Play the recording for students to check their predictions. They check in pairs and feed back to the class.

| Answers

1 don't agree 2 believe 3 haven't 4 Some

Background note

For more information on the flu vaccine, search for 'flu vaccine effectiveness' on the internet.

WHILE LISTENING

LISTENING FOR GIST

3 (◄ 3.4) 👤👥 Elicit from the class who Mark Li and Sandra Smith might be (students in a university debate; medical experts or politicians in a TV debate, etc.). Play the recording for students to complete the exercise. They check in pairs and feed back to the class.

| Answers

1 S 2 S 3 M 4 M 5 S

Background note

Alternative medicine describes practices which some people believe have medical benefits but which are not based on scientific evidence. Examples include *homeopathy* and *acupuncture*.

A *respiratory disease* affects the *respiratory* (breathing) *system*, especially the *lungs*.

LISTENING FOR DETAIL

4 (◄ 3.4) 👤 Students work in pairs to try to remember whether the statements are true or false. Play the recording again for them to check their answers. They check in pairs again and feed back to the class.

| Answers

1 T 2 F 3 T 4 F 5 F 6 F

POST LISTENING

Strengthening your point in an argument

👥 Tell students to close their books. Elicit some possible ways of strengthening your point in an argument, and then tell students to read the information in the box and compare it with their own ideas.

5 👤👥 Students work alone to match the attempts with the explanations. They check in pairs and feed back to the class.

| Answers

1 d 2 c 3 a 4 e 5 b

Optional activity

👤 Students underline the parts of the examples in Exercise 5 that they could use in the debates in the final speaking task.

| Answers

1 All of my colleagues have had the vaccination and none of us have got flu.
2 Dr Smith is absolutely right that many vaccines work very well and that millions of lives have been saved by vaccination.
3 I'd definitely like to challenge the idea that there's no scientific basis for our work — I disagree with Mr Li on that point. Let me tell you more about my work in that area.
4 If someone is vaccinated, and then they happen to become ill, that doesn't mean the vaccination caused the illness.
5 Well, I'm sure Dr Smith is a very good doctor, but I think the flu vaccine package I mentioned earlier is clear.

DISCUSSION

6 👥👥👥 Students discuss the questions in pairs or small groups. For Question 3, encourage them to use some of the phrases and techniques from Exercise 5 to highlight their ideas. After a few minutes, open up the discussion to include the whole class.

| Answers will vary.

CRITICAL THINKING

👥 Go through the final speaking task with the class. Elicit what a *debate* is. You can also check students understand the meaning of *healthcare*. (Medicines and treatment given in hospitals and by doctors.) Elicit how a debate on this topic might work. (One speaker argues in favour of free healthcare; another speaker speaks against free healthcare; the first speaker responds to the second speaker's arguments; finally the second speaker responds to the first speaker's arguments, etc.)

ANALYZE

👥 Go through the information with the class and elicit how a person's background might influence their point of view in a debate. (You have had personal experience of some of the issues, or were brought up in a family or society with particular attitudes to an issue, etc.) Also elicit some examples of personal motivations in a debate (You speak in favour of something because it affects you or your family, etc.) and then professional motivations (You speak in favour of something because it's your job, or because it will help you at work etc.).

1, 2 👥👥 Check that everyone understands what *alternative medicine* is. (See Background note in Listening 2 above.) Students read the information and discuss the questions in pairs. They then compare their ideas with another pair. After a few minutes, open up the discussion to include the whole class.

> Answers will vary.

3, 4 👤👥 Students work alone to decide which speaker said which statement. They check in pairs and feed back to the class.

> **Possible answers**
> M: 1, 4, 5
> S: 2, 3, 6

> **Optional activity**
> 👥 Students work in pairs to take turns to present their own opinions about the statements in Exercise 3. They should try to disagree with each other using the techniques and language from Listening 2, Exercise 5.

APPLY

5 👥 Students discuss the topics in pairs. After a few minutes, open up the discussion to include the whole class.

> **Possible answers**
> 1 ML: It's natural; it's better than modern medicine; SS: It isn't proven to work; it doesn't help you.
> 2 ML: This is what people have always done, and it works; SS: Medicine is much more effective than food.
> 3 ML: They're just trying to make you think you're ill and sell you a cure; SS: It's a valuable way for people to learn about how to treat illnesses.
> 4 ML: Everything you do in your life can make you sicker or healthier, including arranging your furniture; SS: Exercise has been proven to have positive health benefits.
> 5 ML: The fever is a natural part of the illness. You don't need to give the child medicine; SS: Aspirin will help the child feel better.
> 6 ML: This may be a good idea, but clinical treatment may still not work for everyone; SS: This is the best thing we can do to prevent illness and disease.

SPEAKING

PREPARATION FOR SPEAKING

Using persuasive language

👥 Elicit briefly from the class what *persuasive language* might be. Tell students to read the information in the box and find three benefits of using persuasive language. (It calls attention to our main opinions, it invites listeners to think about and agree with our point of view and it makes it more difficult for speakers to disagree with us.)

1 👤👥 Students work alone to match the headings with the examples. They check in pairs and feed back to the class.

> **Answers**
> 1 d 2 a 3 e 4 b 5 c

2, 3 👥👥 Students work in pairs to rewrite the facts as statements. Encourage them to use a wide range of techniques from Exercise 1. If there is time, get them to write two different versions of each fact. Students work with another pair to practise reading their persuasive statements. Again, they should use their intonation and body language to try to sound as persuasive as possible. As a follow-up, ask volunteers to feed back on the most persuasive arguments they heard.

> **Answers**
> Exercises 2 and 3: Answers will vary.

SPEAKING TASK

👥 Point out that this is the same task that students prepared for in the Critical thinking section. Tell them to look at the Task checklist after Exercise 6, so that they know what is expected of them. Elicit from the class where they can find useful language for this type of discussion. (Exercise 1 of the Preparation for speaking section has useful language for all the points on the checklist.) Divide the class into groups and each group into two groups (A and B). Point out that one of the features of debates is that speakers' genuine opinions are not important. The challenge is to be able to come up with good arguments even if you personally disagree with them.

PREPARE/PRACTISE

1, 2, 3 👥 Students work in their teams to plan and prepare for the debate. Point out that an opening statement is not just the first sentence, but the whole of the first part of the debate. You could give them guidelines as to how long that statement should be (e.g. 3–5 minutes). Allow plenty of time for this preparation. They should write notes rather than their arguments in full. Monitor carefully and provide support where necessary. You may need to remind them of the Language checklist, to make sure they stay focused.

4 👥 Before you begin the debate, establish a clear procedure for the timing. This is especially important if you have several debates going on at the same time. For example, you could allow three minutes for each opening statement, a pause of five minutes while teams prepare their counter-arguments, and then three minutes for each counter-argument.

DISCUSS

5, 6 👥 When they are ready, start the debates. Monitor carefully while students are speaking to make notes of the good and bad examples of language that you hear. Pay particular attention to the phrases and structures from this unit. At the end of the debates, give and elicit feedback on the success of the debates and the quality of the arguments. Afterwards, give and elicit feedback on the language used during the debate.

TASK CHECKLIST / OBJECTIVES REVIEW

👥 Students complete the checklist in pairs and then report back to the class. Where they feel they need extra practice, discuss with the class how they can get this. You can also feed back individually to them on how well they are able to do the things in the table, and where they need extra practice.

WORDLIST

👥 Students work in pairs to explain the words in the list to a partner. Afterwards, ask volunteers to explain each word to the class.

REVIEW TEST

See page 101 for the photocopiable Review test for this unit and Teaching tips, page 90 for ideas about when and how to administer the Review test.

ADDITIONAL SPEAKING TASK

See page 119 for an additional speaking task related to this unit.

Write the title of the debate on the board and elicit from the class some ways that a government might try to force people to lead healthier lives (putting fluoride in water supplies to prevent tooth decay, making it the law to vaccinate children against diseases, making overweight people or smokers pay more for their healthcare, etc.). Also elicit some simple arguments for and against the statement, but avoid exploring them at this stage. Give each student a photocopy of the model language on page 119. Divide the class into two groups to plan and practise their opening statements. Make sure they also work to predict the opposing side's arguments. Put students into new groups of four, with two people from Group A and B to hold the debate. Set a time limit to make sure everyone finishes around the same time. At the end of the exercise, ask each new group to report back on the results of the debate.

RESEARCH PROJECT

Create a podcast about deadly diseases

Ask students to think about diseases which used to be very common or deadly, but which are now under control or treatable (smallpox, polio, etc.). Divide the class into groups and ask each group to research one of these diseases, including how it is/was spread, treatment and prevention, and the long-term effects of the illness.

Each group then creates a three-minute podcast of this information to share with other groups. This could be shared in class or using online tools. The podcasts could also be used as the basis for short listening tests, whereby each group prepares one or two tasks for the rest of the class based on their recording.

Learning objectives

👥👥👥 Go through the learning objectives with the class to make sure everyone understands what they can expect to achieve in this unit. Point out that students will have a chance to review these objectives again at the end of the unit.

UNLOCK YOUR KNOWLEDGE

👥 👥👥 Check that everyone understands the meaning of *pay off*. (See Language note.) Students then discuss the questions in pairs or small groups. After a few minutes, open up the discussion to include the whole class.

| Answers will vary

Language note

If a risk or a gamble *pays off*, the benefits turn out to be greater than the costs and it was worth taking the risk.

WATCH AND LISTEN

Video script

ANDES MOUNTAIN TREK

▶ The Andes Mountains in Patagonia rise from sea level to over 4,000 metres. In 2004, Steve Ogle and Chad Sayers went there to go trekking. Trekking is risky. One of the biggest dangers trekkers face is the weather.

Video audio: The way the wind moves in Patagonia … it comes sometimes in fierce gusts … you know, you just can't predict it.

Steve and Chad planned to ski a route across the snow and ice where no one had ever been before. The trip began well.

Video audio: The weather was incredible. It was calm, clear, warm. Uh, it was like paradise.

But in Patagonia, the weather can change suddenly. In a storm, winds can reach speeds of 200 kilometres per hour. Not long into their trip, Steve and Chad saw – and felt – a storm coming.

Video audio: And just like that, it got black.

The wind began to blow. They set up their tent for protection. The wind reached a speed of 160 kilometres per hour. The wind blew the snow

and created a ground blizzard. Steve and Chad were trapped. For three days, the men stayed in the tent as the snow slowly covered it. The situation was dangerous. Their tent was disappearing under the snow and the risk of it collapsing was high, so they had to remove the snow.

Video audio: It was just so powerful.

The men were trapped in their tent for ten more days and the snow continued to bury it.

Video audio: When we were in that tent, and that storm was hitting us so hard, we really felt like we could just disappear out there.

The storm continued for two weeks. The men began to worry about running out of food … but then the storm ended. It had dropped 2.5 metres of snow on the tent. Ground blizzards are not unusual in Patagonia. Chad and Steve certainly now have a clearer understanding of the risks of trekking in the Andes.

PREPARING TO WATCH

UNDERSTANDING KEY VOCABULARY

1 👤👥👥 Elicit from the class where the Andes Mountains are. Students then work alone to complete the matching exercise. They check in pairs and feed back to the class.

| Answers
| 1 e 2 f 3 b 4 a 5 d 6 g 7 h 8 c

Background note

The Andes are the world's longest continental mountain range, extending around 7000 km along the west coast of South America, from Venezuela and Colombia in the north down to Tierra del Fuego in the south of Chile and Argentina.

USING VISUALS TO PREDICT CONTENT

2 👥👥 Elicit from the class where they might find a television listing. (In a newspaper or TV guide). Tell students to read the listing to find out what the programme is about. They then discuss the questions in pairs. After a few minutes, open up the discussion to include the whole class. You may need to check some of the words in the TV listing, especially *go missing*, *relive*, *tragedy*, and *celebrate*.

Possible answers

1 Getting lost, not having enough food, getting frostbite or hypothermia, strong winds, getting buried in the snow, etc.

2 For fun and adventure, to prove that they are tough, because they have a lot of money, etc.

Background note

Patagonia is a large region at the southern end of South America, covering the southernmost provinces of Argentina and Chile.

Optional activity

👥 Write these prompts on the board: *Who, Where, When, Why, How long, End result.* Students work in pairs to discuss what they know and can predict about the content of the programme, using the prompts and the TV guide to help them.

Possible answers

Who: Two trekkers, possibly from South America.
Where: Patagonia in the Andes.
When: We don't know, but possibly in the winter.
Why: They probably went trekking for fun; they probably got trapped because of the snow.
How long: Two weeks.
End result: It didn't result in tragedy – they returned safely home.

WHILE WATCHING

LISTENING FOR GIST

3 ▶️👤👥 Go through the statements with the class to elicit initial predictions. You may need to check they understand the word *avalanche*. Play the video for students to decide if the statements are true or false. They check in pairs and feed back to the class.

Answers

1 T 2 F 3 T 4 T 5 F 6 T

4 ▶️👥 Students work in pairs to try to remember the correct information. They then watch the video a second time to check their ideas and correct the notes. They check in pairs again and feed back to the class.

Answers

1 One of the biggest dangers when trekking in Patagonia is the ~~wind~~ **weather**.
2 At the start of the trip the weather was ~~snowy and windy~~ **calm, clear and warm.**
3 The two men faced winds of ~~200~~ **160** kph.

4 ~~Avalanches~~ **A ground blizzard** buried the men's tent in snow.
5 After ~~ten~~ **three** days, the men had to remove snow from the tent to avoid it collapsing.
6 The total snowfall was ~~five~~ **2.5** metres.
7 The storm lasted for ~~10 days~~ **two weeks**.
8 Ground blizzards ~~are~~ **aren't** unusual in Patagonia.

5 👥👥👥 Students discuss the question in pairs or small groups. After a few minutes, open up the discussion to include the whole class.

Answers will vary.

LISTENING 1

PREPARING TO LISTEN

PREDICTING CONTENT USING VISUALS

1 👥👥👥 Students work in pairs to discuss the photograph and answer the questions. After a few minutes, open up the discussion to include the whole class. Make sure everyone knows the words *dune* and *buggy*. (See Language notes.) Avoid confirming or rejecting students' ideas at this stage, as this will undermine the next exercise.

Possible answers

The risks of the sport could be rolling over in the sand in the buggy, getting caught in a sand storm, crashing the buggy, getting sunburn etc.
The risks could be prevented by driving safely, wearing a harness, wearing a helmet, etc.

Language note

A *dune* is a pile of sand created by the wind. Dunes range in size from a few metres tall to a small hill.

A *dune buggy* (or *beach buggy*) is a vehicle with modified wheels, engine, etc., designed for travelling on open sand.

UNDERSTANDING KEY VOCABULARY

2 👤👥 Students work alone to complete the matching exercise. They check in pairs and feed back to the class.

Answers

1 c 2 f 3 b 4 g 5 h 6 j 7 a 8 e 9 i 10 d

WHILE LISTENING

LISTENING FOR GIST

3 🔊 4.1 👤👥 Go through the questions with the class to make sure everyone understands the words, especially *hazards* (things which are or could be dangerous), *off road*, *encounters*, *collision* and *panic*. For Question 1, you could elicit how a–e could be described as a hazard; for Question 2, elicit what advice students expect the speaker will give before they listen. Play the recording for students to choose the correct answers. They check in pairs and feed back to the class.

> **Answers**
> 1 a; c; e
> 2 a; c; d

Listening for clarification

👥 Tell students to close their books. Elicit from the class why and how a speaker might clarify what they have just said. Then tell them to read the information in the box to compare it with their ideas.

4 🔊 4.1 👤👥 Go through the instructions carefully with the class to make sure everyone fully understands what to do. Play the recording for students to tick the method used. They check in pairs and feed back to the class.

> **Answers**
> 1 summary of the situation
> 2 summary of the situation
> 3 opposite scenario
> 4 opposite scenario

POST LISTENING

5 👤 Go through the examples with the class to make sure everyone remembers what active and passive structures *are*. Tell students that we often use passive structures to give clear and direct orders. Refer students to the work they did on the passive in Unit 1 if necessary. (See Page 15 for Language notes.) Students work alone to rewrite the sentences. They check in pairs and feed back to the class.

> **Answers**
> 2 You are not to wear sandals. / Sandals are not to be worn.
> 3 You are to wear goggles at all times. / Goggles are to be worn at all times.
> 4 You are not to remove the harness. / The harness is not to be removed.

PRONUNCIATION FOR LISTENING

Stress for emphasis

👥 Go through the information in the box with the class. Elicit which part of the information in the box might be described as 'additional' (e.g. the second part of the sentence). Write the following sentence on the board: *New information is often stressed to show it is important.* Elicit which words in this sentence might be stressed, and then underline them for students. (The underlined words are *new*, *stressed* and *important*.)

6 🔊 4.2 👥 Students work in pairs to predict which words and phrases in the sentences should be stressed. Then play the recording for them to check their predictions. They compare their answers in pairs again and feed back to the class.

> **Answers**
> 1 The <u>sand</u> is <u>hot</u>, and you have to be prepared to <u>walk</u>.
> 2 You definitely need good <u>foot protection</u>. Does everyone else have suitable <u>shoes</u>?
> 3 I'm talking about using <u>plenty</u> of <u>sunscreen</u> and wearing <u>sun-protective clothing</u>; clothes that <u>cover</u> your <u>skin</u>.
> 4 If you don't wear a <u>harness</u> when we drive off the road, you <u>bounce around in</u> your seat and you could <u>lose control</u>, or you could <u>fall out</u>.

7 👥 Students work in pairs to practise saying the sentences, paying particular attention to the stress patterns. Monitor and provide support where necessary.

DISCUSSION

8 👥👥 Make sure everyone remembers the meaning of *hazards*. Students discuss the questions in pairs or small groups. After a few minutes, open up the discussion to include the whole class.

> **Answers will vary.**

LANGUAGE DEVELOPMENT

Expressing certainty about future events

👥 Tell students to close their books. Draw a vertical line along the side of the board, labelled with 0% at the bottom and 100% at the top. Elicit how certain (in terms of a percentage) the sentence 'You will have an accident' is. (100%) Elicit a range of ways of expressing the same sentence with different levels of certainty, and write these on the board. You could provide some key words (*will*, *could*, *may*, *might*, *sure*, *certain*, *likely*, *unlikely*, *bound to*, etc.) if students cannot come up with any on their own. Note that there is room for disagreement on the precise percentage of certainty for each structure. Then tell students to look at the information in the box to compare it with their ideas.

Suggested answers

↑	100%	You will have an accident; You're sure to have an accident; You're bound to have an accident; You're certain to have an accident.
		You're likely to have an accident.
	50%	You could/may/might have an accident.
		You're unlikely to have an accident.
↓	0%	You won't have an accident; You're sure not to have an accident; You're bound not to have an accident; You're certain not to have an accident.

Language note

Sentences with *sure*, *bound*, *certain* and *(un)likely* are all examples of a structure called subject-to-subject raising, which learners of English often find difficult to understand. In such structures, the subject of a *that* clause is raised to become the subject of the whole sentence, leaving behind a *to*-infinitive instead of the *that* clause:

- I am sure that **you** will cut yourself ➜ **You** are sure to cut yourself.
- It is unlikely that **you** will fall ➜ **You** are unlikely to fall.

For learners of English, the first structure in each case is easier and more logical than the second.

Note that there is no simple/logical version of the structure with *bound*; we have to use a different word (e.g. *inevitable*) instead.

- It is **inevitable** that **you** will have an accident ➜ **You** are **bound** to have an accident.

Could, *may* and *might* are all used with roughly the same meaning. They can all be strengthened by adding *well* after the verb. (*You could well hurt yourself.*)

EXPRESSING CERTAINTY

1 🧍👥 Students work alone to decide if the statements are certain, probable or possible. They check in pairs and feed back to the class.

> ### Answers
> 1 Poss 2 Poss 3 C 4 C 5 Poss 6 C 7 C 8 Prob

2 🧍👥 Students work alone to put the words in order. They check in pairs and feed back to the class.

> ### Answers
> 1 You could hurt your head so please wear a helmet.
> 2 You're bound to crash into a rock if you keep driving like that.
> 3 You're certain not to get an eye injury if you wear goggles.
> 4 You're unlikely to fall out if you're wearing a harness.
> 5 You're sure to have a collision if you're not concentrating.
> 6 Careful! You may get sunburn if you don't use sunscreen.

ADJECTIVES TO DESCRIBE RISK

3 🧍👥 Students work alone to match the words with the definitions. They check in pairs and feed back to the class.

> ### Answers
> 1 d 2 h 3 a 4 g 5 b 6 f 7 c 8 e

LISTENING 2

PREPARING TO LISTEN

USING YOUR KNOWLEDGE

1 👥👥👥 Check that everyone understands what a *risk assessment* is. (A discussion or a report which analyses the possible risks from a particular situation.) Students then work in pairs to make their lists. After a few minutes, open up the discussion to include the whole class.

> Answers will vary.

2 👤👥 Check students understand the words *scald*, *hob* and *fumes*. They then work alone to match the verbs with the hazards. They check in pairs and feed back to the class.

> **Answers**
>
> 1 d 2 g 3 e 4 b 5 h 6 a 7 f 8 c

Background note

- If you *scald* yourself, you are injured by touching very hot liquid or vapour (e.g. steam).
- A *hob* is the top, flat part of a cooker (or stove), for heating food in pans. The inside of a cooker is called an *oven*.
- *Fumes* are gases or vapours which are unpleasant or harmful to breathe in.

Optional activity

👥 Students work in pairs to describe their own experiences of the eight hazards. They could ask and answer questions using phrases like '*Have you ever …?*' and '*What happened?*'.

WHILE LISTENING

LISTENING FOR GIST

3 🔊 4.3 👤👥 Check that students understand the words *hygiene*, *precautions* and *inspector*. Play the recording for students to choose the best answers to the questions. They compare answers in pairs and feed back to the class.

> **Answers**
>
> 1 a 2 c 3 b

Background note

Hygiene /ˈhaɪ dʒiːn/ refers to the process of keeping a place clean and healthy, particularly in terms of germs and other microscopic dangers.

LISTENING FOR DETAIL

4 🔊 4.3 👥 Go through the table with the class to make sure students understand what is needed in each part of it. Students then work in pairs to try to remember the missing information. Play the recording for them to check their ideas. Make sure they know to take notes while listening, rather than write full sentences. They compare their answers in pairs again and feed back to the class.

Answers

hazard	risk	risk level	risk reduction
falling from height	*major injury*	*low*	*Two people should use the ladder, one climbing, the other holding it. Make sure the floor is dry.*
stove: burns from the hob	major injury	medium	Turn hobs off when not in use.
stove: scalds from hot liquids	major injury	high	Don't fill pots too full.
stove: smoke and fumes	minor injury	high	Use extractor fan.

POST LISTENING

5 👤👥 Students work alone to underline the language in each sentence that indicates the most important information. They check in pairs and feed back to the class.

> **Answers**
>
> 1 First of all 2 The main thing is you need to 3 The most important thing 4 First of all 5 The main thing 6 The most important thing

DISCUSSION

6 👥👥👥 Make sure everyone understands the difference between *hazard* and *risk* in this context. Students discuss the questions in pairs or small groups. After a few minutes, open up the discussion to include the whole class.

> **Answers will vary.**

CRITICAL THINKING

👥👥👥 Go through the task with the class. Check that everyone remembers what a *risk assessment* is. You can also check that they understand the difference between *accidents*, *illnesses* and *injuries*, and some possible examples of each in the context of a *theme park*.

UNDERSTAND

Understanding statistics

👥 Tell students to close their books. Elicit from the class what statistics are. (They may be able to remember they are mentioned in Listening 2.) and why they are used. Then tell students to look at the information in the box to compare it with their ideas.

1 👥 Students cover the table and look only at the title, then discuss the task in pairs. As a follow-up, you could tell them to look at the table to check their predictions. When you check answers with the class, make sure everyone fully understands all the words in the table. (See Background note below.)

> **Answers**
> Information included in the table: 1, 3, 6

> **Background note**
> - In this context, *incidents* is the general name for all accidents, injuries and illnesses.
> - A *theme park* (Disneyland, Legoland, etc.) contains a large number of *attractions* (things that people want to visit) including many *rides* (mechanical attractions that move).
> - A *scrape* is a minor injury that draws blood caused by a flat surface (e.g. a pavement), not a sharp object.
> - If you *trip*, you fall because your foot catches on something and you lose your balance. If you *choke*, you cannot breathe because something (usually food) is stuck in your throat.

2 👥 Students work in pairs to answer the questions and feed back to the class.

> **Answers**
> 1 1,117 2 30.5% 3 3 4 13.2% 5 4,107 6 2,290,010

ANALYZE

INTERPRETING STATISTICS

3, 4, 5 👤👥 Students work alone to answer Exercises 3 and 4. For Exercise 4, point out that their decisions should be based on their own judgements and experiences, not on the information on the percentages of incidents in the table. They compare their answers in pairs and feed back to the class.

> **Answers**
> Exercise 3: 1 minor injuries 2 burn from fireworks
> Exercise 4: Students' own answers, but the first three incidents are generally less serious than the last three in the list.
> Exercise 5: Students' own answers.

APPLY

Understanding anecdotal evidence

👥 Tell students to close their books. Elicit from the class what an anecdote is and what anecdotal evidence might be. Elicit why such evidence can be useful. Then tell students to look at the information in the box to compare it with their ideas.

> **Background note**
> An *anecdote* /ˈænɪkdəʊt/ is a story, usually based on your own experience or the experience of someone you know. Anecdotes are very useful for personalizing an argument and making it memorable, but they need to be treated with care. People often find anecdotal evidence easier to believe than statistical evidence, even though logically we should trust statistics (facts about hundreds or thousands of people) more than stories about one or two people.

6 👤👥 Students decide if the statements are anecdotal or statistical. They check in pairs and feed back to the class.

> **Answers**
> 1 A 2 S 3 S 4 A

7, 8 🔊 4.4 👥 Students work in pairs to rank the injuries. Play the recording for them to check their predictions. They compare their answers in pairs again and feed back to the class.

> **Answers**
> a 3 b 1 c 2

9 🔊 4.4 👥 Students work in pairs to try to remember what was said about each question in the dialogue. Then play the recording again for them to check and to complete their answers. They check again in pairs and feed back.

> **Answers**
> 1 The speaker's brother who worked in a kitchen often cut himself with knives.
> 2 The percentages of injuries caused by wet floors, knives, and hot cooking equipment.
> 3 No, the anecdotal evidence doesn't fully support the statistical evidence.

SPEAKING

PREPARATION FOR SPEAKING

TALKING ABOUT STATISTICAL EVIDENCE

1 🔊 4.5 👤👥 Play the recording for students to complete the sentences. They check in pairs and feed back to the class.

> **Answers**
> 1 4,107 2 0.18% 3 982 people in every thousand
> 4 32.2% 5 1,117 6 five cases per thousand
> 7 27.3% 8 18.4%

2 👥 Students work in pairs and take turns to make sentences about the table using the expressions in bold from Exercise 1. When they are ready, ask volunteers to report back to the class.

> **Answers will vary.**

Language for clarification

👥 Tell students to read the information in the box and elicit examples of expressions to clarify what you have just said. (See Exercise 3 for some possible answers.)

3 👤👥 Students work alone to complete the sentences. Check everyone understands the meanings of *chopping* and *dusty*. They check in pairs and feed back to the class.

> **Answers**
> 1 mean is 2 talking about 3 In other words 4 mean
> 5 say

USING MODALS TO TALK ABOUT HAZARDS AND RISKS

4 👥 Go through the instructions and the example with the class and elicit some examples of phrases for describing causes and effects. (*This may lead to …; This could result in …; This might mean …*, etc.) Students work in pairs to make sentences about the hazards. Encourage them to be creative both in terms of the possible risks and the language they use to describe them. When they are ready, ask volunteers to share their ideas with the class.

> **Answers**
> Answers will vary. See Student's Book for example answer.

EXPRESSIONS FOR TALKING ABOUT LIKELIHOOD AND PROBABILITY

5 👤👥 Students work alone to number the collocations in order. They check in pairs and feed back to the class.

> **Answers**
> 2, 5, 1, 4, 3

> **Language note**
> - Adjectives (like the ones in the table) can be classed as gradable or ungradable. Gradable adjectives (*possible, unlikely*, etc.) typically have comparative and superlative forms, and can be used with adverbs like *very*. Ungradable adjectives describe extremes (e.g. *impossible*) and aren't normally used with comparatives, superlatives or *very*. Some adjectives can be used in two ways (e.g. *I'm very certain* – gradable; *I'm absolutely certain* – ungradable).
> - Adverbs that go with gradable adjectives include: *very, extremely, highly, fairly, really*, etc.
> - Adverbs that go with ungradable adjectives include: *absolutely, totally, really*, etc.
> - *Quite* can go with both types of adjective, with a clear difference in meaning: *It's quite* (absolutely) *impossible; It's quite* (fairly) *unlikely*.

SPEAKING TASK

👥 Point out that this is the same task that students prepared for in the Critical thinking section. Tell them to look at the Task checklist after Exercise 4, so that they know what is expected of them. Elicit from the class where they can find useful language for this type of speaking. (Exercise 4 of Preparation for speaking has work on modals; Exercise 3 has useful language for clarification; Exercise 5 has useful language for talking about likelihood and probability; in the Language development section, there is further work on modals and other ways to describe likelihood and probability and in Listening 1, there is work on using stress for emphasis.)

PREPARE/PRACTISE

1, 2 👥 Go through the instructions with the class. Make sure everyone knows where in the form to fill in the information from the Critical thinking section (in the column marked *risk*). Point out that there are several possible risks for each hazard area. Students work in groups to discuss which risks may occur in which area. They then work in their groups to discuss the risk levels of each situation they have identified.

DISCUSS

3, 4 👥 Check that everyone understands all the words in the anectdotal evidence, especially *leak*, *rubbish bins* and *drinking fountains*. Students work in their groups to discuss their ideas for risk reduction. They then work with another group to compare and amend their answers. Monitor carefully while students are speaking to make notes of good and bad examples of language that you hear. Pay particular attention to the phrases and structures from this unit that students use. To finish the activity you could ask some of the groups to share their answers with the class, explaining any amends they made. Afterwards, give and elicit feedback on the language used during the discussion.

Background note

A *drinking fountain* is a device which provides free drinking water, often in public places.

TASK CHECKLIST / OBJECTIVES REVIEW

👥 Students complete the checklist in pairs and then report back to the class. Where they feel they need extra practice, discuss with the class how they can get this. You can also feed back individually to them on how well they are able to do the things in the table, and where they need extra practice.

WORDLIST

👥 Students work in pairs to explain the words in the list to a partner. Afterwards, ask volunteers to explain each word to the class.

REVIEW TEST

See page 103 for the photocopiable Review test for this unit and Teaching tips, page 90 for ideas about when and how to administer the Review test.

ADDITIONAL SPEAKING TASK

See page 120 for an additional speaking task related to this unit. Give each student a photocopy of the model language on page 120.

Write the phrase 'jungle adventure tours' on the board and elicit from the class what kind of activities a holiday like this might involve, and what some of the hazards might be. Write the hazards on the board. Divide the class into small groups. Students then work in their groups to conduct a risk assessment using the statistics. You could extend the discussion by getting them to discuss risk reduction for the hazards from the board. At the end of the exercise, get volunteers from each group to feed back on the results of their risk assessment.

RESEARCH PROJECT

Create a wiki of some of the riskiest jobs in the world

Divide the class into groups and ask them to make a list of some of the riskiest jobs in the world. When they have thought about this, ask them to search 'world's riskiest jobs' online. Each group researches one of the jobs, including finding out why it is risky and what workers can do to reduce these risks.

Each group then produces a wiki with all these details, using text, images, audio and videos to bring the jobs to life. Search 'create wiki' for how to do this. The class could then vote for which they think is the riskiest job. There are free online voting systems which allow you to do this. Search 'voting software' to view some of them.

5 MANUFACTURING

Learning objectives

👥 Go through the learning objectives with the class to make sure everyone understands what they can expect to achieve in this unit. Point out that students will have a chance to review these objectives again at the end of the unit.

Lead in

👥 In small groups, students look around the classroom (or in their bags) and choose five things that have been manufactured. They then discuss the following questions:

- Which of the things are easy to manufacture?
- Which things are complicated to manufacture?
- Which things couldn't have been manufactured 10/50/100 years ago?
- Which things were made in another country?

After a few minutes, ask volunteers from each group to report back on their discussions to the class.

UNLOCK YOUR KNOWLEDGE

👥👥 Students discuss the questions in pairs or small groups. After a few minutes, open up the discussion to include the whole class.

> Answers will vary.

WATCH AND LISTEN

Video script

BUILDING A RUNNING SHOE

▶ New Balance running shoes are designed using cutting-edge technology, based on the idea of William J. Riley, who started the business in 1906. The original inspiration for the running shoes came from chickens. Riley noticed that chickens have four parts of their feet on the ground at the same time and this gives them stability.

Running puts a lot of strain on many different parts of the body. Today, New Balance use computers to make sure that their shoes support the whole body. The shoes need to be strong enough to take the impact of running, but comfortable enough to give the foot flexibility and speed. They cushion the parts of the foot that hit the ground, but also give the shoes stability, so that the foot is supported.

New Balance perform tests and review feedback from runners, to design the shoes on a computer. They then print in 3D to make a quick full-size model. The 3D printing machine uses information from the computer to heat sand and mould it to make the model. This model will be used to make thousands more shoes that will be sold around the world.

This factory makes 300,000 pairs of shoes a year. The shoe uppers are made by hand. The upper starts with one piece of leather which is cut out into 29 pieces to make the top of the shoe. A robot sews the pieces together, but the logo must be sewn by hand, taking special attention to get it just right. Sewing the upper into three dimensions is a skilled job that can also only be done by human hand. The upper is then ready to be glued to the sole. Finally, the shoes are checked for quality, ready for their laces and box.

New Balance say 'a better fit produces better performance'. It takes testing, design and high-tech manufacturing to make a better fitting shoe.

PREPARING TO WATCH

UNDERSTANDING KEY VOCABULARY

1 👤👥 Students work alone to label the photograph. They check in pairs and feed back to the class.

> **Answers**
> 1 upper 2 laces 3 logo 4 sole

2 👤👥 Students work alone to match the words to the definitions. They check in pairs and then feed back to the class.

> **Answers**
> 1 f 2 b 3 g 4 c 5 a 6 e 7 d 8 h

Optional activity

👤 Use these questions with the class to check and develop students' understanding of the target words:

1 What other very *skilled* jobs can you think of? (Surgeon, watchmaker, etc.)

2 How do you think shoes can help a runner's *performance*? (Comfortable shoes mean the runner can run further; they could also be very light, which means the runner can run faster, etc.)

3 What you think *cutting-edge* shoe design is? (The shoes are designed on a computer and tested using the most modern computer simulations.)

4 In what other situations is *stability* important? (Designing cars, furniture, etc.)

5 What other things need to be *balanced* in sports shoes? (There needs to be a balance between quality and cost; it needs to be easy to take the shoes off, but they mustn't fall off easily, etc.)

6 What other things are sewn together into a *three-dimensional* shape? (A football, leather gloves, etc.)

7 How can you assess the *quality* of a shoe? (It feels comfortable; it looks good; it lasts a long time, etc.)

8 What is the difference between a *high-tech* and low-tech shoe testing process? (A high-tech process might involve computer simulations; a low-tech process might involve getting people to run in the shoes.)

WHILE WATCHING

UNDERSTANDING MAIN IDEAS

3 ▶ 👥 Students work in pairs to predict whether the statements are true or false. Play the video for them to check their predictions. They check in pairs again and feed back to the class.

> **Answers**
> 1 F 2 T 3 F 4 T 5 F

LISTENING FOR KEY INFORMATION

4 ▶ 👤👥 Students work alone to try to match the sentence halves from memory. Play the video again for them to check their answers. They check in pairs and feed back to the class.

> **Answers**
> 1 b 2 f 3 e 4 a 5 d 6 c

5 👥👥👥 Students discuss the questions in pairs or small groups. After a few minutes, open up the discussion to include the whole class.

> **Answers will vary.**

LISTENING 1

PREPARING TO LISTEN

UNDERSTANDING KEY VOCABULARY

1 👤👥 Students work alone to match the words and phrases to the pictures. They discuss their answers in pairs and feed back to the class.

> **Answers**
> a handmade, individually produced, high-quality, small-scale
> b industrial, identical, factory-made, mass-produced

2 👥 Students work in pairs to label the statements. Avoid confirming or rejecting their ideas at this stage, as this will undermine the next exercise.

> **Answers**
> See Exercise 3.

WHILE LISTENING

LISTENING FOR GIST

3 🔊 5.1 👤👥 Play the recording for students to check their predictions from Exercise 2. They check in pairs before feeding back to the class.

> **Answers**
> 1 H 2 H 3 F 4 F 5 H 6 F 7 F 8 F

LISTENING FOR DETAIL

4 🔊 5.1 👤👥 Students work alone to try to match the sentence halves. Then play the recording again for them to check their answers. They check in pairs and feed back to the class.

> **Answers**
> 1 c 2 h 3 g 4 f 5 d 6 e 7 b 8 a

POST LISTENING

Signposting

👥👥👥 Tell students to close their books. Elicit from the class what they think *signposting* is and what it is used for. Elicit situations when signposting language could be especially useful. (A presentation or a lecture, i.e. situations where the listeners do not interact with the speaker.) Students to look at the information in the box and compare it with their ideas.

5 👤👥 Students work alone to match the sentences with the situations. They check in pairs and feed back to the class.

> **Answers**
> 1 b 2 e 3 a 4 c 5 d

| Suggested answers

1 I'll divide the lecture into … parts.
2 The first part of the talk will look at …
3 We've looked at …, but …?
4 Let's turn now to …
5 In short, …

PRONUNCIATION FOR LISTENING

Pauses in prepared speech

👥 Tell students to read the information in the box to find out how prepared speech is different from natural speech. Elicit from the class what *clause boundaries* are (see Language note below).

> Language note
>
> *Clauses* are groups of words built around a verb, often with a subject and objects. Sentences consist of one or more clauses. *Clause boundaries* mark the beginnings and endings of clauses. In written language, they are often marked with punctuation; in spoken language they are often marked with pauses.

6, 7 🔊 **5.2** 👥 Play the example to the class, drawing attention to the pauses in the prepared speech. Students then look at Exercise 7 and work in pairs to predict where the pauses will be in the extract. Play the recording for them to check their predictions.

| Answers

Groups of workers started making identical articles of clothing in high-volumes // using sewing machines. // By the end of the 19th century // lots of everyday items // such as shirts, //trousers // and dresses were mass-produced.

8 👥 Students work in pairs to practise saying the two paragraphs, paying particular attention to the pauses.

DISCUSSION

9 👥 👥 Students discuss the questions in pairs or small groups. After a few minutes, open up the discussion to include the whole class.

| Answers will vary.

⊙ LANGUAGE DEVELOPMENT

MODEL VERBS OF NECESSITY AND OBLIGATION

Modal verbs for necessity and obligation

👥 Tell students to close their books. Elicit what *modal verbs* are and the difference between *necessity* and *obligation*. (See Language note below.) Elicit examples of sentences expressing necessity and obligation using modal verbs, and write them on the board. Tell students to look at the information in the book to compare it with their ideas. Make sure everyone fully understands the difference between *must* and *have to*, and between *mustn't* and *don't have to*. You could elicit who might say each of the example sentences, to make it clear that those with *must/mustn't* would only be spoken by a person with the authority to impose rules.

Language note

- Strictly speaking, there are only nine *modal verbs* in English: *will, would, can, could, may, might, shall, should* and *must*. These verbs are defined according to their specific grammar; for example, they have no third person form, they are followed by infinitives without *to*, they form negatives by adding *not* or *n't* at the end of the verb (e.g. *you mustn't* – not: *you don't must*) and they come at the beginning of yes/no questions (e.g. *Can I help?*; not: *Do I can help?*). There are also a few verbs which sometimes behave like modals, for example *ought, need* and *dare*.

- The term modal is sometimes used to describe verbs with similar meanings to true modals even though grammatically speaking, they are not. (*Have to, be able to, be allowed to, need to*, etc.)

- The difference between *obligation* and *necessity* is rather subtle. *Obligation* is usually associated with rules and regulations (e.g. *You must wear a helmet.*); *necessity* comes from the way the world works. (e.g. *Everyone needs to eat.*)

1 👤👥 Students work alone to circle the correct answers. They check in pairs and feed back to the class.

Answers

1 mustn't 2 doesn't have to 3 mustn't 4 mustn't
5 don't have to

2 👤👥 Students work alone to complete the sentences. Encourage them to use a range of modal verbs in their answers. They compare their answers in pairs and feed back to the class. Note that different answers are possible for most of the sentences.

Answers

1 must / have to / need to
2 mustn't
3 don't need to / don't have to
4 must / have to / need to
5 don't have to / don't need to
6 mustn't

Optional activity

👥 Students work in pairs to write five more sentences using a range of modals to express necessity and obligation. Ask volunteers to read their sentences aloud with the modal verb blanked. The other students in the class have to work out what the missing modal verb should be. (A number of options will probably be possible, as in Exercise 2.)

ACADEMIC VOCABULARY FOR PRODCTION AND PROCESSES

3 👤👥 Students work alone to match the words with the definitions. They check in pairs and feed back to the class.

Answers

1 j 2 i 3 f 4 a 5 h 6 g 7 d 8 b 9 e 10 c

4 👤👥 Check that everyone understands what a *collocation* is (two or more words which often go together with a specific meaning). Students then work alone to identify the incorrect collocation for each word in the right-hand column on the table. They check in pairs and feed back to the class. As a follow-up, you could discuss the meanings of some of the correct collocations with the class. (*Office management, average cost, selection process, fundamental concept*, etc.)

Answers

1 assistant 2 reduced 3 innovative 4 new
5 scientific 6 assistant 7 reduce 8 office

Optional activity

Tell students to look back at the words they circled in Exercise 4. Students work in pairs to identify correct collocations for each of these words from the words in the right-hand column. You may need to do the first one with the class as an example. Note that more than one collocation may be possible in some cases. When they are ready, check with the class.

Suggested answers

1 assistant manager
2 reduced cost / volume
3 innovative method / management / process / approach / concept
4 new method / manager / management / process / approach / concept
5 assistant manager
6 average cost / volume
7 reduce cost / volume
8 office manager / management

LISTENING 2

PREPARING TO LISTEN

UNDERSTANDING KEY VOCABULARY

1 👤👥 Students work alone to match the verbs with the definitions. They check in pairs and feed back to the class. As a follow-up, you could elicit from the class how each verb could relate to a car factory.

> **Answers**
> 1 f 2 c 3 a 4 e 5 b 6 d

PREDICTING CONTENT USING VISUALS

2 👤👥 Students try to complete the diagram. They check in pairs and feed back to the class. You may need to check that they understand the meaning of *rust* (a red-brown substance that damages items made of iron or steel), *sealant* (special material used to seal something) and *coat* in this context (a layer of something, for example, paint). Avoid confirming or rejecting their ideas at this stage, as this will undermine the next exercise.

> **Answers**
> See Exercise 3.

WHILE LISTENING

LISTENING FOR GIST

3 🔊 5.3 👤👥 Play the recording for students to check their answers. They check in pairs and feed back to the class.

> **Answers**
> 1 base coat 2 rust-protection coat 3 sealant
> 4 colour coat 5 clear coat

LISTENING FOR DETAIL

4 🔊 5.3 👥 Students work in pairs to remember as much as they can about the use and purpose of each layer of paint. Make sure they write notes, not full sentences. Play the recording for them to check their ideas and make further notes. They compare their answers in pairs, and listen again if necessary, before feeding back to the class.

> **Possible answers**
> 1 Protects the car from water damage (rust).
> 2 Protects the base coat and increases the protection from water damage.
> 3 Seals the joins, helps the car drive quietly and keeps water out.
> 4 Gives the car colour.
> 5 Protects the colour coat from sun damage and scratches.

> **Language note**
> The verb *count* has many meanings. In Listening 2, the verb is used to mean *not including: The bottom four layers, not counting* (if we don't take into consideration) *the clear coat, use about 3.5 litres of paint altogether.*

POST LISTENING

5 👥 Students briefly discuss the questions in pairs. Discuss the answers with the class.

> **Answers**
> 1 before/after
> 2 so that

6 👤👥 Students work alone to complete the task. They check in pairs and feed back to the class.

> **Answers**
> 1 This second rust-protection coat wouldn't stick to bare metal, but it sticks to the base layer very well, (which is why) the base layer goes on first.
> 2 This sealant is the final layer to be applied before the colour goes on. We do this (so that) the colour layer will cover the sealant.
> 3 After this, the coloured paint is applied. Obviously the colour coat has to go on after the base coat, the rust protection coat and the sealant (because otherwise) you wouldn't see it.

DISCUSSION

7 👥👥👥 Students discuss the questions in pairs or small groups. After a few minutes, open up the discussion to include the whole class.

> **Answers will vary.**

CRITICAL THINKING

👥 Go through the task with the class. Elicit from students whether it is more similar to what they heard in Listening 1 or Listening 2. (It is more similar to Listening 2.)

ANALYZE

Dependency diagrams

👥 Students close their books. Elicit from the class what a *dependency diagram* might be. You could provide a prompt by eliciting what it means if one part of a process *depends* on another. Tell students to look at the information in the book to check their ideas.

1 👥 Students work in pairs to put the steps in the correct order. Note that there are several possible correct orders for the steps. Discuss any variations in orders with the class.

> **Suggested answer**
> 1 c 2 e 3 a 4 g 5 f 6 h 7 b 8 d

2 👥 Students look at the diagram and discuss the questions in pairs. After a few minutes, ask volunteers to report back their answers to the class.

> **Answers**
> 1 The T-shirt must be designed before cutting out the fabric, assembling the front and back or assembling the sleeves; Cutting out the fabric must take place before assembling the front and back or assembling the sleeves.
> 2 Assembling the front and back and assembling the sleeves could be done in any order. This is shown by the fact that they are in line with each other on the diagram.

APPLY

3 👤👥 Students work alone to complete the diagram. They check in pairs and feed back to the class.

> **Answers**
> 1 add label 2 finish neck 3 add pocket 4 attach sleeves to body

UNDERSTAND

4 👥 👥👥 Students discuss the questions in pairs. After a few minutes, open up the discussion to include the whole class.

> **Possible answers**
> 1 designing the shirt, cutting out the fabric, assembling the front and back, assembling the sleeves, attaching the sleeves, finishing the neck
> 2 adding the label, adding the pocket
> 3 Ironing and packaging the T-shirts, dyeing the fabric, packing T-shirts into boxes for transport and creating other T-shirt designs could all be added to the diagram.
> 4 Packaging, ironing and transporting the T-shirts would have to come later in the process. Adding additional designs could be at several stages, but probably before making the T-shirts. Dyeing the fabric would have to come before it is cut.

SPEAKING

PREPARATION FOR SPEAKING

Explaining processes

👥👥 Students close their books. Check that everyone remembers how the passive voice is formed, and when it is used. Elicit from the class why the passive is useful in explaining processes. (Often when we are explaining a process, we are more interested in what is happening than who made it happen.) Tell students to look at the information and examples in the box to check their ideas.

1, 2 🔊 5.4 👤👥 Students work alone to rewrite the sentences. With weaker classes, you may need to pre-teach the past participles of the verbs, especially *to sew* (*sewn*). Tell them not to use the word *by* in their answers. When they are ready, play the recording for them to check their answers. Students to then practise saying the sentences with a partner.

> **Answers**
> 1 Firstly, the client is measured.
> 2 Then the style and fabric of the suit are chosen.
> 3 Next, the pieces are cut out and sewn together to make the suit.
> 4 When the suit is ready, the fit is checked and altered as necessary.
> 5 Finally the suit is worn.

EXPLAINING DEPENDENCY IN A PROCESS

3 👤👥 Students work alone to complete the table. They check in pairs and feed back to the class.

Answers

first steps	next steps	things that happen at the same time	results and consequences	final steps
Firstly Initially The process starts with First of all To begin with	then next after that afterwards after later the next step	at the same time meanwhile simultaneously	as a result consequently so subsequently	finally last of all

Stressing words that indicate order

👥 Elicit from the class some very simple instructions for making tea (no more than three sentences) and write these on the board. Make sure students use some words to indicate order in their sentences. Then elicit from the class which words from the sentences on the board they might stress in the sentences. (Possible answer: <u>First</u>, put some water in a kettle to boil. <u>Then</u> put a tea bag into a cup. <u>Finally</u>, pour boiling water into the cup.) Tell students to read the information in the box and compare it to their ideas.

4, 5 🔊 5.5 👥 Students work in pairs to predict which words should be stressed. Then play the recording for them to check their ideas. They check in pairs and feed back to the class. Students practise saying the sentences with a partner, paying particular attention to the stressed words.

Answers

2 before 3 after 4 at the same time as 5 Meanwhile

6 👥 Students work in pairs to describe the process of making coffee, using the diagram to help them. Encourage them to use a wide range of words/phrases from Exercise 3 in their descriptions. Afterwards, ask volunteers to share their ideas with the class.

SPEAKING TASK

👥 Point out that this is the same task that students prepared for in the Critical thinking section. Tell them to look at the Task checklist after Exercise 4, so that they know what is expected of them. Elicit from the class where they can find useful language for this type of speaking. (Exercise 3 in the Preparation for speaking introduced a wide range of adverbs and other words for indicating the order of steps; the Language development section focused on modals to talk about dependency; Exercise 1 in the Preparation for speaking section for speaking focuses on using the passive to explain processes; Exercise 5 focuses on stressing words that indicate order.)

Optional lead-in

👥 Students work in small groups to brainstorm a wide range of things which are made by hand or in a factory. When they are ready, tell them to cross out from their lists any items whose process would be too complicated to explain. Then tell them to cross out any items whose process is extremely simple, i.e. contains fewer than 6 steps. Elicit the remaining items from each group and write them on the board. Students can then choose one of the items from the board for the focus of their speaking task.

PREPARE

1, 2 👤 Students work alone to answer the questions and to make notes of their answers. They draw a dependency diagram for their process and plan which phrases from the Preparation for speaking section to use in their presentation.

PRACTISE/DISCUSS

3, 4 👥 Students work in pairs to describe their processes to each other and to take notes. Make sure they know to take notes in this exercise, as they will need to use them to describe the same processes later. They then use these notes to repeat their partners' descriptions. Monitor carefully while students are speaking to make notes of good and bad examples of language that you hear. Pay particular attention to the phrases and structures students use from this unit. As a follow-up, ask some volunteers to describe their own processes for the whole class. Afterwards, give and elicit feedback on the language used during the description of the process.

TASK CHECKLIST / OBJECTIVES REVIEW

👥 Students complete the checklists in pairs and then report back to the class. Where they feel they need extra practice, discuss with the class how they can get this. You can also feed back individually to them on how well they are able to do the things in the table, and where they need extra practice.

WORDLIST

👥 Students work in pairs to explain the words in the list to a partner. Afterwards, ask volunteers to explain each word to the class.

REVIEW TEST

See page 105 for the photocopiable Review test for this unit and Teaching tips, page 90 for ideas about when and how to administer the Review test.

ADDITIONAL SPEAKING TASK

See page 121 for an additional speaking task related to this unit.

Choose an object in the classroom (e.g. a computer monitor) and elicit from the class how it could be recycled. Encourage students to guess the process. Write useful vocabulary on the board, especially verbs for disassembling an object (*remove*, *take off*, *take apart*, *unscrew*, *separate*, etc.). Give each student a photocopy of the model language on page 121. Students work alone to draw a dependency diagram of an object of their choice and plan how to describe the process. To make this easier, you could brainstorm a list of suitable objects with the class first. When they are ready, put them into pairs to describe their processes and take notes on their partner's process. Students then describe their partner's process back to them based on their notes.

Finally, ask volunteers to report back to the class.

RESEARCH PROJECT

Present a diagram to show how something is made

Divide the class into groups and ask them to think about how something is made, (processed food, technology, materials, etc.). They could also research how environmentally friendly the manufacturing process is. Students could use the tools online to record and share their research.

Using a slideshow or presentation app, ask each group to present diagrams of the steps involved in their manufacturing process. The presentations could be shared as videos on a video-sharing website.

6 ENVIRONMENT

Learning objectives

👥👥 Go through the learning objectives with the class to make sure everyone understands what they can expect to achieve in this unit. Point out that students will have a chance to review these objectives again at the end of the unit.

Lead-in

👥👥 Write the following questions on the board for students to discuss in small groups.

1 What does the word *environment* mean to you?

2 What are some examples of threats to the environment (a) in your country, (b) in other countries?

2 Do you think it is important for us to protect the environment? Why / Why not?

3 Do you do anything to help the environment?

UNLOCK YOUR KNOWLEDGE

👥👥👥 Make sure everyone understands all the words in the questions, especially *deforestation* (cutting down or destroying forests), *consequences* and *natural resources*. Students then work in pairs or small groups to discuss the questions. After a few minutes open up the discussion to include the whole class.

| Answers will vary.

WATCH AND LISTEN

Video script

ORANGUTAN CONSERVATION

▶ Orangutans live in the rainforests of Malaysia and Indonesia. Unfortunately, the orangutan is an endangered species. Today, there are fewer than 35,000 orangutans in the wild.

Human activities, such as logging, have destroyed the orangutans' habitat. Cutting down trees often kills adult orangutans, leaving the baby animals as orphans. New roads and growing towns and villages have also destroyed the orangutans' habitat. More than 80% is now gone forever. However, conservationists are working to save the orangutans. They are rescuing them and returning them to the rainforest.

This orangutan lives at a rescue centre in Indonesia. More than 200 orangutans live in this rescue centre. The workers here prepare the orangutans for their return to the wild. Most of these orangutans came here because their natural habitat was destroyed to create more farm land or cut down for wood.

Some of these baby orangutans are only four weeks old. Their parents may have been killed, or captured and sold as pets. Babies normally stay with their parents until they are about six years old, so they would be vulnerable in the wild on their own.

Before the orangutans can return to the wild, they must learn basic survival skills. Every day, they are taken to the forest so they can learn and practise how to be a wild orangutan. The orangutans love practising the skills they need to live in their natural habitat. They practise climbing, swinging and even drinking.

So while some people destroy the orangutans' habitat, others are dedicated to helping them learn the skills they need to survive. If these beautiful and endangered animals are going to survive in the wild for years to come, they will need all the human help they can get. Only then will orangutans survive in the Asian wilderness.

PREPARING TO WATCH

USING YOUR KNOWLEDGE TO PREDICT CONTENT

1 👥 Check that everyone understands the word *habitat*. (The type of place where a particular species of animal or plant naturally lives.) Students then discuss the questions in pairs. Elicit some answers from the class.

| Possible answers
|
| 1 Building roads, expanding villages/towns/cities, building dams to make lakes, polluting the air/water/soil, etc.
| 2 Humans want to increase the size of cities, harness more natural resources, etc.
| 3 Use less resources, protect local animals, etc.

UNDERSTANDING KEY VOCABULARY

2 👤👥 Students work alone to match the words to the definitions. They check in pairs and feed back to the class.

| Answers
| 1 d 2 h 3 a 4 g 5 e 6 b 7 f 8 c

Background note

Apes are a group of mammals which includes chimpanzees, gorillas, orangutans and humans. Unlike most monkeys, apes have no tail.

Tropical forest is defined as a forest lying in the region between the Tropic of Cancer and the Tropic of Capricorn, close to the equator, where it is hot all year round.

Optional activity

👥 Use these questions with the class to check and extend students' understanding of the key words in Exercise 2:

1 Why is *logging* bad for the environment? (It destroys animals' natural habitats and it means there are fewer trees to absorb carbon dioxide.)

2/3 What is the *orangutan's* natural *habitat*? (They live in tropical rainforests.)

4 Can you think of any other *endangered species*? (Tiger, mountain gorilla, blue whale, giant panda, etc.)

5 Where do *conservationists* work? (Some work with animals in the wild to protect their habitats, protect them from dangers, etc.; others work in animal hospitals or offices, where they are involved in activities like raising money to save local environments.)

6 Which countries in the world have *rainforests*? (Malaysia, Indonesia, Papua New Guinea, Sri Lanka, Congo, Cameroon, Brazil, etc.)

7 What do you think happens in an animal *rescue centre*? (People look after baby animals whose parents have died and they help prepare animals to be released back into the wild.)

8 Why might people want to *capture* an orangutan? (They might want to sell it as a pet or as food; they might want to help it, for example by giving medicine, etc.)

WHILE WATCHING

UNDERSTANDING MAIN IDEAS

3 ▶👤👥 Tell students to read the three sentences and ensure that they know that they are only listening for the main idea of the video. Play the video for them to choose the correct sentence. They check in pairs and feed back to the class.

| Answers
| Sentence 2 best gives the main idea of the video.

Background note

Orangutans live on only two islands in South East Asia: Sumatra (which is part of Indonesia), and Borneo (which is governed by Brunei, Indonesia and Malaysia).

An *orphan* is a child whose parents have died. The adjective *orphaned* describes a child (or an animal) who has become an orphan.

LISTENING FOR KEY INFORMATION

4 ▶👤👥 Students try to remember the answers to the questions. You may need to check that they understand the meaning of the words *vulnerable*, *swinging* and *orphaned*. (See Background note above.) Play the video again for students to check their ideas. They check in pairs and feed back to the class.

| Answers
| 1 fewer than 35,000
| 2 more than 80%
| 3 Their habitats were destroyed to create farmland or for wood.
| 4 They rescue them and then return them to the forest.
| 5 Cutting down trees kills their parents.
| 6 They need to practise skills they will need in the wild, such as climbing, swinging and drinking.

DISCUSSION

5 👥👥 Students discuss the questions in pairs or small groups. After a few minutes, open up the discussion to include the whole class.

| Answers will vary.

LISTENING 1

PREPARING TO LISTEN

UNDERSTANDING KEY VOCABULARY

1 👤👥 Students work alone to read the text and complete the matching exercise. They check in pairs and feed back to the class.

> **Answers**
>
> 1 a 2 d 3 e 4 b 5 c 6 d

Distinguishing main ideas from details

👥 Tell students to read the information in the box. Elicit why it is useful for a listener to be able to distinguish main ideas from details when someone is talking. (The listener needs to be able to organize the information he/she receives, so it is important to know what is a new topic and what is simply additional information about the current topic.)

2 👤👥 Students work alone to identify the two sets of sentences. They check in pairs and feed back to the class.

> **Answers**
>
> Sentences 1–6 are main ideas, Sentences a–f are details.

3 👤👥 Students work alone to complete the matching exercise. They can compare answers in pairs, but avoid confirming or rejecting their ideas at this stage, as this will undermine the next exercise.

> **Answers**
>
> See Exercise 4.

WHILE LISTENING

LISTENING FOR MAIN IDEAS

4 🔊 6.1 👤👥 Play the recording for students to check their answers to Exercise 3. They check in pairs and feed back to the class.

> **Answers**
>
> 1 c 2 d 3 b 4 a 5 f 6 e

LISTENING FOR DETAIL

5 🔊 6.1 👤👥 Play the recording for students to complete the notes. They check their answers in pairs and feed back to the class.

> **Answers**
>
> 1 10,000 2 rainforest 3 nine million 4 160, 000
> 5 Africa and Asia 6 stealing food 7 wildlife 8 tribes
> 9 conservationists 10 pollution

POST LISTENING

6 👤👥 Students work alone to choose the statements that best match the lecturer's opinion. They check in pairs and feed back to the class.

> **Answers**
>
> 1 a 2 b 3 a

PRONUNCIATION FOR LISTENING

SENTENCE STRESS

7 🔊 6.2 👤👥 Go through the instructions with the class. Play the recording of the first two sentences, to make sure that everyone can hear the differences in stress and understands how this affects the meaning of the sentences. Play the rest of the recording for students to mark the stress on the sentence halves. They check in pairs and feed back to the class.

> **Answers**
>
> 3 Humans have changed the <u>Earth</u> …
> 4 <u>Humans</u> have changed the Earth …
> 5 Humans <u>have</u> changed the Earth …
> 6 Humans have <u>changed</u> the Earth …

8 👤👥 Students work alone to match the sentence halves. They check in pairs and feed back to the class.

> **Answers**
>
> 1 e 2 b 3 c 4 a 5 d 6 f

9 👥 Students practise saying the sentences in pairs, paying particular attention to sentence stress. When they are ready, ask volunteers to read the sentences aloud to the class.

Optional activity

👥 Tell students to work in pairs. Ask them to find and underline examples of sentences with contrastive stress in sentences from the Video script and Listening 1 you have written on the board (see below). Discuss with the class which words they would stress in the sentences.

Suggested answers

Video script:

- So while <u>some</u> people <u>destroy</u> the orangutans' habitat, <u>others</u> are dedicated to <u>helping</u> them learn the skills they need to survive.

Listening 1:

- Just 10,000 years ago, about <u>half</u> of the planet was covered in ice. Today it's around <u>10%</u>.
- Part of this environmental change is due to <u>natural</u>, rather than <u>human</u> causes.
- There were originally <u>16</u> million square kilometres of rainforest worldwide. <u>Nine</u> million remain today …
- Humans haven't only affected <u>the land</u> and its animals; they have also affected <u>the sea</u>.
- We tend to think of human activity as always having a <u>negative</u> impact on the environment. However, some people feel that we can have a <u>positive</u> impact too.

DISCUSSION

10 👥 👥 Students discuss the questions in pairs or small groups. After a few minutes, open up the discussion to include the whole class.

Answers will vary.

⊙ LANGUAGE DEVELOPMENT

PREPOSITIONS

Complex prepositions

👥 Tell students to close their books. Elicit from the class what a preposition is and what a complex preposition might therefore be. Students then look at the information in the explanation box and the examples in the table in Exercise 1 and compare them with their ideas.

Language note
- A *preposition* is a grammatical word like *in, at, by* or *from*. Prepositions can be followed by noun phrases (e.g. *in the forest*), pronouns (e.g. *from* or *it*), or *-ing* verb forms (e.g. *by eating*).
- *Complex prepositions* are prepositions made of two or more words: *in front of, on top of, instead of, according to, out of, because of, in addition to, in spite of, on behalf of*, etc.

1 👥 Students work alone to match the headings to the complex prepositions in the table. They check in pairs and feed back to the class.

Answers
1 c 2 a 3 e 4 d 5 b

2 👥 Students work alone to circle the correct preposition. They check in pairs and feed back to the class.

Answers
1 Based on 2 due to 3 According to 4 instead of 5 as well as 6 except for

VERBS TO DESCRIBE ENVIRONMENTAL CHANGE

3 👥 Students work alone to match the words with the definitions. They check in pairs and feed back to the class.

Answers
1 f 2 g 3 d 4 h 5 b 6 a 7 c 8 e

4 👥 Students work alone to complete the sentences. You may want to point out the prepositions *to* and *from* after the gaps in sentences 1 and 4. They check in pairs and feed back to the class.

Answers
1 adapted 2 survived 3 declined 4 extracted 5 impacted 6 affected 7 occurred 8 exploited

LISTENING 2

PREPARING TO LISTEN

UNDERSTANDING KEY VOCABULARY

1 👤👥 Students work alone to match the words with the definitions. They check in pairs and feed back to the class.

> **Answers**
> 1 f 2 e 3 c 4 d 5 g 6 h 7 b 8 a

> **Optional activity**
>
> 👥 Use the following questions to check and extend students' knowledge of the key vocabulary:
>
> 1 What other things have a *surface*? (A table, a lake, etc.)
>
> 2 Where in the world might you expect to see a *dust storm*? (Dust storms are especially common in deserts such as the Sahara, but they occur in all dry regions of the world, such as parts of the US, China and Australia.)
>
> 3 What are some examples of *minerals* which occur naturally in the Earth's surface? (Quartz, marble, diamond, granite, graphite, etc.)
>
> 4 What are *diamonds* used for? (To make jewellery and in industrial cutting and polishing tools.)
>
> 5 What objects are made of *copper*? (Pots, wires, pipes, etc.)
>
> 6 What are some *sources* of oil? (We can extract oil from under the ground and produce it from plants, such as olives or sunflowers.)
>
> 7 Do you use *natural gas* in your home?
>
> 8 What are some products of the *mining* industry? (Coal, gold, diamonds, etc.)

WHILE LISTENING

LISTENING FOR MAIN IDEAS

2 🔊 6.3 👤👥 Check students understand all the words in the exercise, especially *saltier* (containing more salt) and *acacia*. (See Background note below.) Play the recording for students to choose the correct answers. They check in pairs and feed back to the class. Note that for Question 2, the speaker discusses the survival of a way of life, but not of humans themselves, which is why the correct answers are c and d.

> **Answers**
> 1 a; c
> 2 c; d
> 3 a; c

> **Background note**
>
> • *Irrigation* is the artificial process of bringing water to agricultural land, which would otherwise be too dry to grow crops.
>
> • A *city-dweller* is a person who lives in a city. The verb *dwell* is an old word meaning *live*.
>
> • The speaker mentions *ground surface temperatures* of 80°C, which refers to the temperature at ground level in direct sunlight.
>
> • *Acacia* /əˈkeɪʃə/ trees grow in warm and hot countries around the world. They usually have thorns and edible seeds.
>
> • An *oryx* /ˈɒrɪks/ is a species of antelope. Oryxes have long, straight horns and pale fur. An Oryx can be seen in the logo for Qatar Airways.

LISTENING FOR DETAIL

3 🔊 6.3 👥 Students work in pairs to try to remember the order of the facts. Play the recording again for them to check. They compare their answers in pairs again and feed back to the class.

> **Answers**
> 1 c 2 e 3 f 4 h 5 g 6 a 7 b 8 d

POST LISTENING

LISTEN FOR TEXT ORGANIZATION FEATURES

4 👤👥 Students work alone to match the parts of the presentation with the sentences. They compare their answers in pairs and feed back to the class. When you check with the class, you could elicit the order of the three parts of the presentation in Listening 2 (1 background; 2 problem; 3 solution).

> **Answers**
> 1 a 2 b 3 c

5 Students work alone to identify the parts of the talk. They check in pairs and feed back to the class.

> **Answers**
> a 3 b 2 c 1

Optional activity

Write the following words and phrases from Listening 2 in two columns on the board. Students work in pairs to make collocations. They could check their answers in the script on page 212, or listen to recording again. In class feedback, make sure everyone understands all the collocations.

1 threats	a areas
2 background	b available
3 harsh	c dwellers
4 a deep	d environment/conditions
5 city-	e information
6 a wide	f life
7 stable	g soil
8 wilderness	h to this environment
9 way of	i understanding
10 freely	j variety

> **Answers**
> 1 h 2 e 3 d 4 i 5 c 6 j 7 g 8 a 9 f 10 b

DISCUSSION

6 Students discuss the questions in pairs or small groups. After a few minutes, open up the discussion to include the whole class.

> **Answers will vary.**

CRITICAL THINKING

Go through the task with the class. Discuss briefly how the task is similar to and different from the presentation in Listening 2. (It is similar in that both talks focus on the destruction of deserts; it is different because it focuses specifically on the Sahara desert rather than deserts in general.)

ANALYZE

Organizing information in a presentation

Students close their books. Elicit from the class how understanding the organization of information in a presentation might be useful. Tell students to look at the information in the book and compare it to their own ideas.

1 Students work alone to label the columns. They check in pairs and feed back to the class. Note that the example/detail labels could swap positions.

> **Answers**
>
> | introduction | background | main idea | example/ detail | detail/ example | solution |
> |---|---|---|---|---|---|

2 Students work alone to decide if the statements are true or false. They check in pairs and feed back to the class.

> **Answers**
> 1 T 2 T 3 F 4 F 5 T 6 F

CREATE

3, 4 Tell students to work alone to create the outline for their talk. With weaker classes, you could point out that the first two points are the main ideas, the next five words and phrases are examples, and the rest of the information is details. Monitor carefully while students are creating their outlines, offering language support if necessary. When they are ready, they compare their outlines in pairs. Finally, discuss students' outlines with the class.

> **Answers**
> Answers will vary according to the information prioritized by students in their talk outlines.

SPEAKING

PREPARATION FOR SPEAKING

Signposting language in a presentation

👥 Elicit from the class what *signposting language* is and why it is useful. Students read the information in the box and compare it with their own ideas.

1 👤👥 Students work alone to match the phrases in bold with their purposes in a presentation. They check in pairs and feed back to the class.

> **Answers**
> 1 e 2 g 3 d 4 f 5 c 6 a 7 h 8 b

2 👤👥 Students work alone to complete the matching exercise. They check in pairs and feed back to the class.

> **Answers**
> 1 c 2 f 3 d 4 h 5 a 6 e 7 g 8 b

Giving background information and explaining a problem

👥 Students close their books. Elicit from the class why it is important to include background information in a presentation and how this background information can be organized. Then tell students to read the information in the box to compare it with their ideas.

3 👤👥 Students work alone to match the items with their purposes. They check in pairs and feed back to the class.

> **Answers**
> 1 a 2 b 3 e 4 c 5 f 6 d

SPEAKING TASK

👥 Point out that this is the same task that students prepared for in the Critical thinking section. Tell them to look at the Task checklist after Exercise 5, so that they know what is expected of them. Elicit from the class where they can find useful language for this type of speaking (Exercises 1, 2 and 3 of the Preparation for speaking section and the final exercises for Listening 1 and Listening 2.)

PREPARE

1, 2, 3 👥 Students work in small groups to discuss the information and to plan their presentations. Allow plenty of time for this preparation stage. Monitor carefully and provide language support and guidance as students write their ideas in the chart. You may need to explain some of the words in the fact file. (See Background notes below.)

> **Background note**
> - *Grazing* is the name for the activity when animals eat grass. *Overgrazing* happens when too much grass is eaten in an area, and it does not grow back. When this happens, grassland can quickly turn to desert.
> - A *windbreak* is something which provides shelter from the wind.

> **Optional activity**
> 👤 You could encourage students to conduct their own research online, either in class or as a homework task, and to use this research in their presentations.

PRACTISE/DISCUSS

4, 5 👥 Students work in their groups to practise their presentations. They then form new groups to deliver their presentations. Monitor carefully while students are speaking to make notes of the good and bad examples of language that you hear. Pay particular attention to the phrases and structures students use from this unit. When they have finished, the groups discuss the similarities and differences between the various presentations. Afterwards, give and elicit feedback on the language used during the presentations.

TASK CHECKLIST / OBJECTIVES REVIEW

Students complete the checklists in pairs and then report back to the class. Where they feel they need extra practice, discuss with the class how they can get this. You can also feed back individually to them on how well they are able to do the things in the table, and where they need extra practice.

WORDLIST

Students work in pairs to explain the words in the list to a partner. Afterwards, ask volunteers to explain each word to the class.

REVIEW TEST

See page 107 for the photocopiable Review test for this unit and Teaching tips, page 90 for ideas about when and how to administer the Review test.

ADDITIONAL SPEAKING TASK

See page 122 for an additional speaking task related to this unit.

Write the speaking task on the board. Elicit from the class what they know or can guess about the Antarctic environment (its climate, wildlife, threats to the environment and measures to protect it, etc.). Divide the class into groups of around four students. Give each student a photocopy of the model language on page 122. In their groups, students use the fact file to plan a presentation, following a similar format to the one at the end of Unit 6. If you have computers with internet access in the classroom, students could conduct their own research. If this is not possible, you could allow them to invent any details and examples they need. When students have prepared and practised their presentations, put them into new groups to deliver them. At the end of the exercise, you could ask students to report back on the presentations that they heard. (What was interesting; what they learned, etc.)

RESEARCH PROJECT

Create a website about an environmental threat

Ask students to make a list of different environmental problems and then decide on one which they consider may be a real threat to them (desertification, flooding, droughts, destruction of trees, loss of biodiversity, etc.). Students could use tools online to share and discuss their ideas.

Students create a class website outlining the causes and dangers of their chosen environmental threat, as well as what can be done about it (search 'create free website'). They could include audio clips, videos and images on the website.

7 ARCHITECTURE

Learning objectives

👥 Go through the learning objectives with the class to make sure everyone understands what they can expect to achieve in this unit. Point out that students will have a chance to review these objectives again at the end of the unit.

Lead in

👥 On the board, write *Architectural Wonders of the World*. Elicit briefly from the class what the phrase means. Students work in small groups to brainstorm a list of ten examples of architectural wonders. When they are ready, ask volunteers from each group to present their ideas to the class. Discuss with the class similarities and differences between their lists. If some students have never heard of some of the wonders, ask the student who suggested it to explain what it is and why it is so special.

UNLOCK YOUR KNOWLEDGE

👥👥👥 Students work in pairs or small groups to discuss the questions. After a few minutes, open up the discussion to include the whole class.

Answers will vary.

Background note

The building is the Niterói Contemporary Art Museum, in the city of Niterói in Brazil. It is 16 metres high and 50 metres wide.

WATCH AND LISTEN

Video script

CHANGING CHINA

▶ Beijing, the capital of China, is home to over 20 million people. With more than 2000 years of history, the city is of world-class architectural importance and boasts internationally famous sites such as The Great Wall, The Temple of Heaven and The Forbidden City.

The Forbidden City was built in the early 1400s and is an example of traditional Chinese palace architecture. It is a World Heritage site and listed by UNESCO as the largest collection of ancient wooden structures in the world. It is also regarded as the best-preserved palace complex in existence and attracts around eight million visitors per year.

The Great Wall of China stretches for over 8000 kilometres from Shanhaiguan to Lop Lake. It crosses mountains, spans plains and passes through vast deserts. This astonishing miracle of engineering took over 2000 years to build. The Great Wall was built to protect the Chinese Empire against enemies. Thousands of watchtowers stretch as far as the eye can see.

These brick towers are two or three-storeys high. On the top of each one there is a small room shaped like a ship, known as Loulu in Chinese. Today, the history of innovative Chinese architecture and construction lives on.

But there is increasing pressure on architects to accommodate the growing populations of large Chinese cities. The solution is often to construct high-rise buildings, which are fast and economical to put up. China is a county of architectural contrast, with landmarks ranging from the Forbidden City to the more recent Bird's Nest stadium, built for the 2008 Olympic Games.

Traditional housing, like the beautiful *hutongs* or the more recent *shikumen*, is fortunately being preserved for future generations to enjoy.

From the ancient past to exciting modern developments … China's architectural wonders have helped it become one of the most popular tourist destinations in the world.

PREPARING TO WATCH

UNDERSTANDING KEY VOCABULARY

1 👤👥 Students work alone to match the words with the definitions. They check in pairs and feed back to the class.

Answers
1 d 2 f 3 g 4 c 5 b 6 h 7 e 8 a

2 👤👥 Students work alone to complete the sentences. They check in pairs and feed back to the class.

Answers
1 brick 2 complex 3 landmark 4 heritage 5 preserve 6 construction 7 development 8 structure

WHILE WATCHING

UNDERSTANDING MAIN IDEAS

3 ▶ 👤👥 Students read through the sentences and predict the correct expressions for each sentence. Play the video for them to check their ideas. They check in pairs and feed back to the class.

> **Answers**
>
> 1 traditional 2 Lop Lake 3 housing developments
> 4 preserved

> **Background note**
>
> • The *Forbidden City* was the home of Chinese emperors for 500 years. The name comes from the fact that people were not allowed to enter or leave the city without the Emperor's permission.
> • *Shanhaiguan* (or the *Shanhai Pass*) is the place where the Great Wall of China meets the ocean, 300 kilometres east of Beijing.
> • *Lop Lake* was a salt lake between two deserts in the west of China. It has now largely dried up.
> • The *Temple of Heaven* is a large complex of religious buildings in Beijing.
> • *World Heritage Sites* are places (man-made or natural) of particular cultural or architectural importance to the world. *UNESCO* (*The United Nations Educational, Scientific and Cultural Organization*) maintains a list of almost a thousand World Heritage Sites.
> • The *Bird's Nest* is a nickname for the national stadium in Beijing, designed for the 2008 Olympic Games.
> • A *hutong* is a narrow street common in Beijing.
> • *Shikumen* is a traditional architectural style that combines elements of Chinese and European architecture common in the city of Shanghai.

UNDERSTANDING DETAIL

4 ▶ 👥 Students work in pairs to try to remember if the statements are true or false. Play the video again for them to check their ideas. They check their answers in pairs and feed back to the class.

> **Answers**
>
> 1 F 2 T 3 F 4 T 5 F 6 T 7 F

DISCUSSION

5 👤👥 Students discuss the questions in pairs or small groups. After a few minutes, open up the discussion to include the whole class.

> **Answers will vary.**

LISTENING 1

PREPARING TO LISTEN

UNDERSTANDING KEY VOCABULARY

1 👤👥 Elicit from the class what a *property developer* is. (See Background note below.) Students look at the diagram and label it with the words in the box. They check their answers in pairs and feed back to the class.

> **Answers**
>
> 1 original features 2 supporting walls 3 extension
> 4 steel 5 beams 6 glass 7 stone 8 foundations
> 9 concrete

2 👤👥 Students look at the labelled diagram and write the words in the correct column in the table. They check their answers in pairs and feed back to the class.

> **Answers**
>
> | building materials | architectural features |
> | --- | --- |
> | concrete | foundations |
> | steel | extension |
> | glass | beams |
> | stone | supporting walls |
> | | original features |

> **Background note**
>
> • A *property developer* is a person or company that invests money into improving existing buildings and constructing new ones, with the aim of selling them for a profit.
> • In older buildings, *beams* were long, strong pieces of wood used to construct ceilings and roofs. In modern architecture, beams are often made of steel.
> • The *original features* of a building are window frames, fireplaces, etc. which remain from the time the building was constructed.
> • The *foundations* of a building are the underground structures which ensure that it is stable.
> • In modern buildings, there are two types of wall: *supporting walls* are thick and strong enough to support the weight of the roof above them; *partition walls* serve only to separate rooms within a building, so they do not need to be thick or strong.

USING YOUR KNOWLEDGE

3 👥 Students work in pairs to discuss the questions. When you check answers with the class, you could write a list of building materials on the board and ask students to add them into the table in Exercise 2.

| Answers will vary.

WHILE LISTENING

LISTENING FOR MAIN IDEAS

4 (◄) 7.1) 👤👥 Students read the sentences and predict what the speakers will decide to do. Play the recording for them to check their ideas. They check in pairs and feed back to the class.

| **Answer**
| Sentence 1 is the correct answer.

LISTENING FOR DETAIL

5 (◄) 7.1) 👥 Students work in pairs to try to correct the notes. You may need to check they understand the word *regeneration*, *contemporary* and *refurbishment*. (See Background note below.) Then play the recording again for them to check their answers.

| **Answers**
| 1 The developers **dis**agree that a new development in Westside is a good idea.
| 2 There isn't any regeneration going on in Westside.
| 3 There has**n't** been a lot of investment in the area in the past 20 years.
| 4 The developers think that the best idea would be to ~~knock down the warehouse~~ **use/keep the warehouse and put modern features on it.**
| 5 The developers decide ~~that they need to choose between~~ **to combine** a contemporary building style and a traditional one.
| 6 The building can**'t** offer floor space for shops.
| 7 The shop units would mostly be on the ~~second~~ **ground** floor, **with flats above.**
| 8 Refurbishment would mean ~~removing all~~ **keeping some of** the original features.

Background note

- *Regeneration* is a process where city planners encourage economic development in old, poor or rundown areas, usually in a city.
- A *contemporary* style is modern and up-to-date.
- *Refurbishment* is the process of improving the inside of a building, for example by painting and decorating it, adding new furniture and fittings, etc.

POST LISTENING

Understanding analogies

👥 Students close their books. On the board, write the phrase *The room was as cold as ice*. Elicit the literal and intended meanings of this *analogy* (/əˈnælədʒi/). Elicit from the class why analogies are useful. Students read the information in the box to compare it with their ideas.

6, 7 👥 👥 Students work in pairs to match the analogies with the meanings and discuss the questions in Exercise 7. When you check answers with the class, make sure everyone fully understands the literal and intended meanings of all the analogies.

| **Answers**
| Exercise 6
| 1 b 2 d 3 c 4 a
| Exercise 7
| Analogies 1 and 3 are negative and support knocking the old building down, 2 and 4 are positive and support converting and modernizing the building.

Background note

Literally, a *lease* is a contract which gives you permission to use somebody else's property in exchange for money. So if you get *a new lease on* your flat, you are allowed to live there for a new, extended period of time. If you are given *a new lease on life* (or *of life*), you feel as if you have been given the chance to live longer. In other words, you feel younger and more energetic.

8 👥 Students work in pairs to practise using the analogies in Exercise 6. When they are ready, ask some volunteers to present their analogies to the class.

PRONUNCIATION FOR LISTENING

Emphasis in a contrasting opinion

👥👥 Tell students to read the information in the box. You could elicit some examples of emphasis in a contrasting opinion by making statements which are clearly incorrect and inviting students to correct you, paying particular attention to stress. (*I don't think it's <u>cold</u> today; actually I think it's quite <u>hot</u>.*, etc.)

9 🔊 7.2 👤 👥👥 Students read through the sentences to predict which words might be stressed and listen to the first example. Play the recording for them to check their answers. They check in pairs and feed back to the class.

> ### Answers
> 2 A: It has some beautiful features.
>   B: It looks as though it's about to <u>collapse</u>!
> 3 A: Acquiring such an old building could be a mistake.
>   B: I think the project could be a <u>great success</u>.
> 4 A: It would be more of a transformation if we built a modern building made of materials like steel and glass.
>   B: We'll maintain more of a connection to the past if we include the <u>old building</u> as part of the <u>new one</u>.

10 👥👥 Students work in pairs to practise reading the sentences, paying particular attention to stress.

DISCUSSION

11 👥👥 👥👥👥 Students work in pairs or small groups to discuss the questions. After a few minutes, open up the discussion to include the whole class.

> Answers will vary.

◉ LANGUAGE DEVELOPMENT

VERBS WITH FUTURE MEANING

Verbs with future meaning

👥👥 Tell students to close their books. On the board, write the sentence *We'll finish soon.* Elicit from the class a range of other ways of expressing this using future forms (*We're going to finish soon; We're finishing soon; We finish soon; We might finish soon; We expect/hope/plan to finish soon;* etc.) and the differences in meaning between them. Tell students to read the information in the box to find out which future forms are the focus of the next section.

> ### Language note
> There are many ways of expressing the future in English, and the differences between them are rather subtle – several future forms are usually possible to express one idea.
> - *We'll finish soon* may be used to make a subjective prediction (i.e. one based on the speaker's opinion), a promise, a spontaneous decision, etc.
> - *We're going to finish soon* may be used to make an objective prediction (based on evidence) or to describe a decision made earlier.
> - *We're finishing soon* is used to describe a plan seen as more or less certain.
> - *We finish soon* is used to describe a future fact, as determined by a schedule, for example.
> - *We may/might finish soon* is used to make a tentative prediction.
>
> The vast majority of verbs with a future meaning (the subject of Exercise 1) are followed by a *to*-infinitive (*plan, intend, expect,* etc.). There are also a handful of verbs with a future meaning followed by an *-ing* form (*envisage, anticipate, look forward to* etc.), but these are much less common. Some verbs with a future meaning are also followed by a *that* clause or a noun phrase, (e.g. *predict* or *foresee*).

1 👤 👥👥 Students work alone to complete the sentences. They check in pairs and feed back to the class.

> ### Answers
> 1 to begin 2 constructing 3 to consult 4 keeping
> 5 to call 6 to have 7 to visit 8 to meet

2 👤 👥👥 Students work alone to make sentences from the prompts. They check in pairs and feed back to the class.

> ### Answers
> 1 He hopes to study law at university.
> 2 She plans to live in the UK
> 3 She promises to send you an email.
> 4 They anticipate taking university entrance exams next year.
> 5 I expect to see Fawaz in the library.
> 6 We intend to start construction on the project next weekend.

ACADEMIC VOCABULARY FOR ARCHITECTURE AND TRANSFORMATION

3 Students work alone to complete the matching exercise. They check in pairs and feed back to the class.

> **Answers**
> 1 b 2 e 3 c 4 f 5 h 6 g 7 a 8 d

4 Students work alone to complete the table. They check in pairs and feed back to the class.

> **Answers**
>
> | verb | noun |
> |---|---|
> | *anticipate* | anticipation |
> | *contribute* | contribution |
> | *maintain* | maintenance |
> | *transform* | transformation |
> | abandon | *abandonment* |
> | convert | *conversion* |
> | *acquire* | acquisition |
> | expand | expansion |

5 Students work alone to complete the sentences. They check in pairs and feed back to the class. You could draw attention to the useful phrase in sentence 3: *make a vital contribution.*

> **Answers**
> 1 expand 2 transform 3 contribution 4 anticipate
> 5 conversion 6 acquire 7 abandon 8 maintain

LISTENING 2

PREPARING TO LISTEN

USING YOUR KNOWLEDGE

1, 2 Check that everyone understands what a *housing development* is. Students then work in pairs to discuss possible solutions to the four problems. When they are ready, put them with another pair to compare answers. Finally, open up the discussion to include the whole class.

> **Answers will vary.**

UNDERSTANDING KEY VOCABULARY

3 Students work alone to complete the matching exercise. They check in pairs and feed back to the class.

> **Answers**
> 1 h 2 f 3 d 4 a 5 c 6 g 7 e 8 b

4 Students work in pairs to describe the pictures in Exercise 5, using as many of the words from Exercise 3 as possible. When they are ready, ask volunteers to share some of their descriptions to the class.

> **Answers will vary.**

WHILE LISTENING

LISTENING FOR GIST

5 (◀) 7.3 Tell students to predict which description might go with which picture. Play the recording for them to check their ideas. They check answers in pairs and feed back to the class.

> **Answers**
> 1 c 2 d 3 a 4 b

LISTENING FOR DETAIL

6 (◀) 7.3 Students work with a partner to try to remember if the developers or the clients made the statements. You may need to check they understand *households*, *reflective glass*, *viable* and *come up with*. They then listen a second time to check their answers. They check in pairs again and feed back to the class.

> **Answers**
> 1 D 2 D 3 C 4 C 5 C 6 C 7 D 8 D

POST LISTENING

Making suggestions

Tell students to close their books. Write the phrase *We should ask for more time* on the board. Elicit from the class some ways of making the suggestion stronger (e.g. *We really need to ask for more time; It's essential that we ask for more time*, etc.) and ways of making it more tentative (e.g. *Why don't we ask for more time? We could consider asking for more time*, etc.). Tell students to look at the information in the box and compare it with their own ideas.

7 Students work alone to decide if the statements are strong or tentative. They compare their ideas in pairs and feed back to the class.

| Answers
1 T 2 S 3 T 4 S 5 T 6 S

DISCUSSION

8 Students discuss the questions in pairs or small groups. Encourage them to use a range of strong and tentative language in their discussions, especially for Question 3 (where they need to make suggestions). After a few minutes, open up the discussion to include the whole class.

| Answers will vary.

CRITICAL THINKING

Go through the task with the class. Use the following questions to get students to engage with the topic:

• What are some examples of petroleum companies? (*BP*, *Shell*, etc.)

• Why might a petroleum company own an apartment block for workers? (Because they often send engineers to other countries to extract and refine oil and gas.)

• Why do you think the apartments feel cramped and uncomfortable? (Because they are too small for the number of people who live in them.)

• Why do you think international schools important in places like this? (Because many international workers would not take a job where their family went with them unless they could guarantee a good education for their children.)

• Why do you think the company needs the workers to move out of the current block? (Because it is now unsuitable, or someone has decided to buy it.)

REMEMBER

1 Students work in pairs to come up with a list of requirements for the accommodation. After a few minutes, open up the discussion to include the whole class. Write their ideas in a list on the board.

| **Suggested answers**
1 The development must:
• house 200 single people and 50 families
• be near international schools
• be near the worker's main offices
• be available within one year
• cost less than $3.8 million.

ANALYZE

2 Students work in pairs to analyze the three solutions. You may need to check students' understanding of the words *storey* and *recreational*.

| Answers will vary.

EVALUATE

3 Students work with another pair to compare answers and discuss the questions. Encourage them to use a range of verbs with future meanings in their discussions, as well as strong and tentative language. After a few minutes, open up the discussion to include the whole class. Note that they will have a chance to discuss the three solutions more fully in the Speaking section, so there is no need to come up with a perfect solution at this stage, only initial ideas to solve the problem.

| Answers will vary.

SPEAKING

PREPARATION FOR SPEAKING

PRONUNCIATION FOR SPEAKING

Emphasizing a word or idea to signal a problem

Students close their books. Write on the board the phrase *Emphasizing a word or idea to signal a problem*. Elicit from the class what this might mean. Then tell students to look at the information in the box to compare it with their ideas.

1, 2 (�))**7.4**) 👥 Students listen to the sentences and underline the word that is emphasized. They then match the sentences with the explanations. They check in pairs and feed back to the class.

Answers

Exercise 1:
1 The <u>main</u> issue is that most retailers don't want to do business here.
2 The main <u>issue</u> is that most retailers don't want to do business here.
3 The main issue is that most <u>retailers</u> don't want to do business here.
4 The main issue is that most retailers don't want to do <u>business</u> here.
Exercise 2:
1b 2d 3a 4c

Optional activity

👤 Students work in pairs to take turns to read the sentences from Exercise 1 in a mixed up order to their partner, who has to listen and provide the correct explanation for the emphasized word.

Presenting a problem

👥 Tell students to close their books. Elicit from the class a range of phrases for presenting a problem. Then tell them to read the information in the box to compare it with their ideas. Draw attention to the literal and metaphorical meanings of the phrase 'We need to find a way around …'. (Literal: there is something blocking our path, and we need to get past it; metaphorical: we have a problem, and we need to find a solution.)

3 👤👥 Students work alone to put the words in order. They check in pairs and feed back to the class.

Answers

1 We need to find a way around the problem of high prices.
2 The problem is that we don't have enough time.

3 The main issue is that local people don't like our design.
4 We need to find a way around the problem of attracting business.
5 The main issue is that the building is collapsing.
6 The problem is that no one wants to live in the area.

Making polite suggestions

👥 Tell students to close their books. Elicit some phrases for making polite suggestions, including statements (*I think we should …* etc.) and questions. (*Why don't we …?* etc.) Then tell them to read the information in the box to compare it with their ideas.

4 👤👥 Students work alone to write suggestions. They check in pairs and feed back to the class.

Answers

1 Could we increase the budget?
2 Can I suggest we increase the budget?
3 Should we consider increasing the budget?
4 How about increasing the budget?
5 Have you thought about increasing the budget?
6 Why don't we increase the budget?

5 👥 Students work in pairs to make suggestions. Encourage them to use a range of structures from Exercise 4. When they are ready, ask volunteers to present their ideas to the class. As a follow-up, you could ask them to repeat the exercise without looking back at the useful language in Exercise 4.

Answers will vary.

RESPONDING TO SUGGESTED SOLUTIONS

6 👤👥 Students work alone to complete the exercise. They check in pairs and feed back to the class. As a follow-up, you could draw attention to the collocation *to address a problem/issue* (deal with or try to solve a problem/issue). You could also elicit the tentative phrase *I'm not sure it addresses the problem*.

Answers

1 rejecting 2 accepting 3 accepting 4 rejecting
5 rejecting 6 accepting

7 👥 Students work in pairs to practise accepting or rejecting the suggestions. Encourage them to use a range of phrases from Exercise 6 in their responses.

Answers will vary.

SPEAKING TASK

👥 Point out that this is the same task that students prepared for in the Critical thinking section. Tell students to look at the Task checklist after Exercise 5, so that they know what is expected of them. Elicit from the class where they can find useful language for the discussion. (All the points covered in the Preparation for speaking section will be useful for the task.)

PREPARE

1 👥 Divide the class into groups of four. Make sure each group chooses one of the solutions – this doesn't have to be their preferred solution, but simply one that can be analyzed in the task. Ideally, each group will look at a different solution.

PRACTISE

2, 3, 4 👥 Divide the groups into pairs and assign roles for each pair. Students plan and practise their presentations or questions in their pairs. Encourage them to use the useful language from the unit in their discussions as well as in the presentations they are preparing. For the developers' presentations, they should make notes for what they will say, rather than writing out a script. Monitor carefully to provide support and guidance as students are working.

DISCUSS

5 👥 When they are ready, put the original groups of four back together to discuss the problem and solution as a group. Make sure everyone has plenty of opportunities to speak. Monitor carefully while students are speaking to make notes of the good and bad examples of language that you hear. Pay particular attention to the phrases and structures students use from this unit. Afterwards, give and elicit feedback on the language used during the discussion.

Optional activity

👥 As a follow-up, ask volunteers from each group to present their improved solutions to the class. You could then open up a class discussion to decide which improved solution is best, again encouraging students to use the target language from this unit.

TASK CHECKLIST / OBJECTIVES REVIEW

👥 Students complete the checklists in pairs and then report back to the class. Where they feel they need extra practice, discuss with the class how they can get this. You can also feed back individually to them on how well they are able to do the things in the table, and where they need extra practice.

WORDLIST

Students work in pairs to explain the words in the list to a partner. Afterwards, ask volunteers to explain each word to the class.

REVIEW TEST

See page 109 for the photocopiable Review test for this unit and Teaching tips, page 90 for ideas about when and how to administer the Review test.

ADDITIONAL SPEAKING TASK

See page 123 for an additional speaking task related to this unit.

Describe the situation in the speaking task to the class and elicit what facilities the university faculty might need, and how it might go about creating the new buildings. Give each student a photocopy of the model language on page 123. Divide the class into groups of four, and each group into two pairs. Allocate the roles of project developers and university representatives to each pair. In their pairs, students plan and practise their presentations and predict questions the other pair might ask. Put the two pairs together to discuss the problem and potential solutions. At the end of the exercise, you could ask volunteers to present their negotiated solutions to the class.

RESEARCH PROJECT

Create a gallery of architecture for an exhibition

Ask groups of students to research different types of 'green' or 'eco' architecture by searching 'green buildings' or 'green architecture', noting down as many features of these buildings as they can. Students could use online tools to share their research.

Each group should then choose a particular building they discovered during their research. Ask them to find out why the building was built and what makes it special. Tell them that the class will be setting up an exhibition to present their building to the public. Students will need to decide how to present the information, who to invite, and how they can make the exhibition interactive for visitors (enable visitors to vote for their favourite building, provide a downloadable audio tour, etc.).They then present their gallery of ideas to the class.

8 ENERGY

Learning objectives

👥👥👥 Go through the learning objectives with the class to make sure everyone understands what they can expect to achieve in this unit. Point out that students will have a chance to review these objectives again at the end of the unit.

Lead-in

👥👥👥 Tell students to imagine that we live in a world without electricity, i.e. all our electrical appliances have stopped working suddenly and permanently. Students work in small groups to discuss the possible impacts of this change on our lives. You could use these questions to focus their attention:

- What would happen in the first week after this change?
- What would happen in the first year after this change?
- What would happen 20, 50 or 100 years after this change?

When they are ready, ask volunteers from each group to present their ideas to the class.

Suggested answers

- In the first week, life for most people would probably be difficult but not dramatically different from normal life. They would have to go out less, and use alternative sources of light and heat, such as fires and candles. They would have to walk, cycle or use animals for transport, because cars, trains etc. would no longer work. Hospitals would shut down so diseases would spread.
- In the first year, life would change dramatically and completely. Supplies of food, fuel and other essential products would run out, especially for people in cities. People would need to start growing their own food to deal with this.
- 20, 50 or 100 years after this change, we might expect to see some recovery, as people organized themselves and found new ways of generating energy.

UNLOCK YOUR KNOWLEDGE

👥 👥👥 Students work in pairs to discuss the questions. After a few minutes, open up the discussion to include the whole class.

Background information

The first car was the Benz Patent-Motorwagen, invented by Carl Benz in 1886, but cars only started to become a popular means of transport after the launch of Henry Ford's *Model T* in 1908.

Answers will vary.

WATCH AND LISTEN

Video script

WATER POWER

▶ California, where the majority of the USA's fresh food is grown, has perfect weather and soil for growing crops. However, the state experiences one major problem – it doesn't get enough rain. The solution to this lack of rain has been to dam the precious few rivers and redirect them to lands thousands of miles away that get as little as eighteen centimetres of rain per year.

Building dams also means creating reservoirs, which are artificial lakes. Lake Mead, in the USA, is an example of this. The lake is 180 kilometres long. It was formed between 1931 and 1936 when Hoover Dam was built. The dam is 220 metres tall, 379 metres wide and 200 metres thick at its base. It controls floods, provides water for farms and generates electricity from flowing river water.

The water enters the dam through these towers and falls more than 200 metres. The falling water turns the turbines inside the dam. As the water falls, the pipes become smaller and the water flows faster. The water is travelling nearly 100 kilometres per hour when it reaches the turbines.

The turbines turn these shafts 180 times per minute. The shafts are attached to generators, which produce massive electrical currents.

Hydroelectric power provides about 24% of the world's electricity, but dams can cause problems, too. A quickly-formed reservoir can destroy animal and plant habitats. In hot, dry places, water can evaporate quickly from lakes, making the water saltier. When water is stored in a reservoir its temperature also changes and when the water is released, it may be too hot or cold for some plants and animals to survive.

Rivers are powerful natural forces. Dams borrow some of that power, so we can turn it into electricity and power our world.

PREPARING TO WATCH
UNDERSTANDING KEY VOCABULARY

1 👤👥 Students work alone to match the words to the definitions. They check in pairs and feed back to the class. You may need to check the pronunciation of *reservoir* /ˈrezəvwɑː/ and the meaning of *rod* (something that is a long, thin cylinder shape, such as a pencil or a fishing rod).

| Answers
| 1 c 2 a 3 d 4 b 5 f 6 g 7 e

Background note

Most *generators* work by moving a loop of wire between the poles of a magnet, which generates an electric current in the wire. Electricity generation usually involves two steps: firstly, a process to create spinning motion, such as sending a high-pressure gas through a turbine; secondly, that the spinning motion is transmitted, via a series of shafts, to the magnet inside the electricity generator itself. See:

http://science.howstuffworks.com/environmental/energy/hydropower-plant.html

for an accessible explanation of how hydropower plants work.

2 👤👥 Students work alone to complete the diagram. They check in pairs and feed back.

| Answers
| 1 generator 2 turbine 3 dam 4 shaft 5 pipe
| 6 reservoir 7 tower

Optional activity

👥 Use these questions with the class to check and extend students' understanding of the key words in Exercise 1:

• Are there any famous *dams* or *reservoirs* in your country?

• How do you think *generators* and *turbines* work? (See Background note, above.)

• Where can you find *pipes* and *shafts*? (You can find pipes inside the walls or under the floor of buildings; you can find shafts inside a car, where they are used to transmit movement from the engine to the wheels, etc.)

• Where can you find *towers*? (In castles, prisons, etc., where they enable guards to have a good view of the ground below; some structures such as skyscrapers and radio masts could also be described as towers.)

WHILE WATCHING
UNDERSTANDING MAIN IDEAS

3 ▶👤👥 Students read through the statements to predict whether they are true or false. Check the meaning of *hydroelectric power* (electrical power generated by the movement of water through a turbine). Play the video for students to check their predictions. They check in pairs and feed back to the class.

| Answers
| 1 F 2 T 3 T 4 F

Background note

The *Hoover Dam* cuts across the Black Canyon of the Colorado River, on the border between the US states of Arizona and Nevada. It was named after US President Herbert Hoover. Lake Mead, which was created by the Hoover Dam, is the largest reservoir in the USA by volume.

LISTENING FOR KEY INFORMATION

4 ▶👤👥 Students read through the information to try to remember the order it appears in the video. Play the video again for students to check their answers. They check in pairs and feed back to the class.

| Answers
| a 3 b 1 c 2 d 4 e 7 f 6 g 8 h 5

DISCUSSION

5 👥👥 Students discuss the questions in pairs. After a few minutes, open up the discussion to include the whole class.

| Answers will vary.

LISTENING 1

PREPARING TO LISTEN
USING YOUR KNOWLEDGE

1 👤👥 Students work alone to complete the fact file. Check the meaning of *mainland* (part of a country or continent which is not an island) and *claim to fame* (the reason why

somebody or something is famous). Students check in pairs and then feed back to the class.

Answers
1 government 2 population 3 area 4 mainland

> **Background note**
> - *El Hierro* /el yero/ is the smallest and the most remote of the Spanish Canary Islands, in the Atlantic Ocean, off the coast of Africa.

2, 3 👥 Students work in pairs to discuss the four questions. After a few minutes, put them with another pair to compare their answers.

Answers
Answers will vary.

WHILE LISTENING

LISTENING FOR GIST

4 🔊 8.1 👤👥 Tell students to read through the sentences and options to predict the answers before they listen. Play the recording for them to check their predictions. They compare their answers in pairs and feed back to the class.

Answers
1 c 2 a 3 c

> **Background note**
> - The power generation system on El Hierro is a good example of *pumped-storage hydroelectricity*. Pumped storage is a technique for managing variations in power supply and demand. At times of high power supply and low demand, water is pumped to a higher level and stored. At times of low power supply and high demand, the water is released, generating more electricity as it flows downhill.
> - A *barrel of oil* is equal to 42 US gallons, or almost 160 litres. This measurement is commonly used in the oil industry for quantities of oil.
> - As explained in the recording, a *dormant volcano* is one that is no longer active and is unlikely to erupt again soon.
> - *Desalination* is the process of removing salt from seawater to leave fresh water. The simplest form of desalination involves boiling the water so it evaporates into steam and can be collected, leaving behind a residue of salt.

LISTENING FOR DETAIL

5 🔊 8.1 👥 Students work in pairs to try to remember the missing information. Play the recording again for them to complete the sentences. They check again in pairs and feed back to the class.

Answers
1 2,000 kilometres; Africa 2 40,000 3 30%
4 3,500 5 dormant volcano 6 Wind turbines
7 generators 8 drinking water; agriculture

> **Optional activity**
> 👥👥 Write the following extracts from the recording on the board:
> 1 *I should have left the city when I was a much younger man.*
> 2 *You may have noticed we have a lot of wind on El Hierro.*
> Elicit from the class the grammatical connection between the two sentences and what they both mean.

> **Suggested answers**
> Both sentences contain the structure modal verb + *have* + past participle. This is a way of combining the meaning of modal verb with an event that happened in the past (underlined below).
> Sentence 1 means "*I regret that I <u>didn't leave</u> the city*".
> Sentence 2 means "*It is possible that you <u>noticed</u>*".

POST LISTENING

LISTENING FOR TEXT ORGANIZATION FEATURES

Understanding digressions

👥👥 Tell students to close their books. Elicit from the class what a *digression* is. (Something that you say or write, which is not directly relevant to the main topic being discussed.) Elicit why people digress, and why it is useful to be able to notice other people's digressions when listening. Students read the information in the box to compare it with their ideas.

6 👤👥 Students work alone to decide if the topics are relevant or digressions. They check in pairs and feed back to the class.

Answers
1 R 2 D 3 D 4 D 5 D 6 R

7 Students complete the matching exercise. They check in pairs and feed back to the class. When you check their answers, elicit why each digression is not relevant to the main topic.

> ### Answers
> 1 b; iii
> Sentence iii is related to the topic of power sources, but does not answer the question.
> 2 c; i
> The first part of sentence i (*My children think it's boring here*) is relevant to the question, but the second part (*I wanted them to grow up the freedom to explore outside.*) is not directly relevant to that question.
> 3 a; ii
> Sentence ii is about what the speaker *doesn't miss*, but the interviewer asked him what he *does miss*.

PRONUNCIATION FOR LISTENING

Intonation related to emotion

8 (◀ 8.2) Go through the instructions with the class and check that everyone understands the five emotions. Play the recording, pausing after each example, and ask volunteers to repeat the sentence with the same emotion. As a follow-up, students work in pairs to practise saying the sentence with the five emotions.

> ### Language note
> Unlike other types of intonation, intonation for emotion is similar for speakers of all languages. However, emotional intonation may be more musical in some languages than in others. Speakers of some languages may create the impression that they are annoyed if they speak with very flat intonation, for example.

9 (◀ 8.3) Play the recording for students to circle the correct emotions. They check in pairs and feed back to the class.

> ### Answers
> 1 sadness 2 excitement 3 excitement
> 4 surprise 5 annoyance

10 Students work in pairs to say the sentences with a range of emotions and guess their partner's intended emotion. Afterwards, you could ask some volunteers to 'perform' their sentences for the class.

DISCUSSION

11 Students discuss the questions in pairs or small groups. You could encourage them to include some deliberate digressions while they are talking, which their partner or the other people in the group try to notice, along with a range of emotional intonation. Afterwards, ask students to report back to the class on any digressions or emotional intonation that they noticed.

> ### Answers will vary.

⊙ LANGUAGE DEVELOPMENT

CONNECTING IDEAS BETWEEN SENTENCES

1 Students work alone to match the phrases with the functions. They check in pairs and feed back to the class.

> ### Answers
> 1 c 2 a 3 b

2 Point out the two parts to this task: adding the titles from Exercise 1 and the expressions from the box. Students work alone to complete the exercise. They check in pairs and feed back to the class.

> ### Answers
>
> | You never feel like you can really relax. | What's more, *In addition, Moreover Furthermore* | my career was in banking, which is an especially stressful job. |
> |---|---|---|
> | **comparing and contrasting** | | |
> | It's a real challenge living here. | On the other hand, *Even so Nevertheless* | we all love it. |
> | **explaining a result** | | |
> | We're a long way from the mainland, | so *therefore as a result* | deliveries always take a few days. |

> **Suggested answers**
>
> The following expressions are especially formal: *furthermore, moreover, nevertheless*.
> The following expressions are rather formal, but still sometimes used in spoken English: *as a result, in addition, therefore*.
> The following expressions are common in natural spoken English: *even so, on the other hand, so*.

3 👥 Students work in pairs to connect the sentences using a range of expressions. When they are ready, ask volunteers to report back some of their answers to the class.

> **Possible answers**
>
> 1 City life is stressful. On the other hand, island life is relaxing.
> 2 The houses use solar electricity. Furthermore, they have water recycling systems.
> 3 Hydroelectric dams can damage habitats. As a result, they have to be planned very carefully.
> 4 The wind blows for 30% of the year. Nevertheless that isn't enough to provide all of the island's electricity.
> 5 This electric car can go 100 kilometres per hour. Moreover, the battery can be charged using solar power.
> 6 The system requires that water moves from a high place to a lower place, so we've placed a water tank on a hill.

ACADEMIC VOCABULARY FOR NETWORKS AND SYSTEMS

4 👤👥 Students work alone to match the words with the definitions. They check in pairs and feed back to the class.

> **Answers**
>
> 1 j 2 i 3 a 4 f 5 e 6 d 7 h 8 b 9 c 10 g

5 👥 Go through the first section in the table to make sure everyone understands how the exercise works. Elicit the meaning of some of the collocations, e.g. *face a challenge, the challenge ahead*. Students then work in pairs to add the remaining words from Exercise 4 to the table. When you check answers with the class, make sure everyone understands the meanings of all the collocations.

> **Answers**
>
> 1 challenge 2 source 3 capacity 4 network
> 5 element 6 volume 7 function 8 potential 9 decline
> 10 generation

6 👤👥 Students work alone to write five sentences using the collocations. After they have read their sentences to a partner, ask volunteers to share their best ideas with the class.

> **Answers will vary.**

LISTENING 2

PREPARING TO LISTEN

USING YOUR KNOWLEDGE

1 👥 Discuss briefly with the class what a *chaired meeting* might be. (A meeting led by one person, who is the *chair*.) Students then work in pairs to discuss the questions. When they are ready, open up the discussion to include the whole class.

> **Possible answers:**
>
> 1 Computers, lights, photocopiers, printers, coffee machines, etc.
> 2 Turn off screens on computers when not using them, turn off lights when no one is in a room, etc.

2 👤👥 Students work alone to read the text and match the words with the definitions. They check in pairs and feed back to the class.

> **Answers**
>
> 1 a 2 g 3 e 4 h 5 d 6 f 7 b 8 c

WHILE LISTENING

LISTENING FOR GIST

3 (◄) 8.4 👤👥 Students read through the statements to check they understand them. Play the recording for them to decide if the statements are true or false. They check in pairs and feed back to the class.

> **Answers**
> 1 T 2 F 3 F 4 T

LISTENING FOR DETAIL

4 (◄) 8.4 👤👥 Students read through the sentences and try to correct them before they listen again. Play the recording for students to check and complete the exercise. They check in pairs and feed back to the class.

> **Answers**
> 1 The team want to find **both big and small solutions** to office energy consumption.
> 2 Energy-efficient light bulbs take a **short** time to make cost savings.
> 3 The windows are too **dirty** to let in enough daylight.
> 4 They might **remove** a photocopier.
> 5 It **would** be a good idea to market the business as green.
> 6 It **might be impossible** to put a solar energy system on the roof of the building.

POST LISTENING

LISTENING FOR OPINION

Persuasive techniques

👥 Tell students to close their books. Elicit from the class ways in which we might try to persuade somebody to do something or to agree with us. They then read the information in the book to compare it with their ideas.

5 👤👥 Check that everyone understands the meaning of *reservations* (concerns that a plan or idea may not work as well as expected). Students work alone to match the sentences with the techniques. They may need to look at the script on page 215/216 to find the sentences in order to understand the context in which they are used here. They check in pairs and feed back to the class.

> **Answers**
> 1 b 2 d 3 a 4 e 5 c

6 👥 Students work in pairs to match the statements to the techniques. Check answers with the class.

> **Answers**
> 1 d 2 c 3 e 4 b 5 a

DISCUSSION

7 👥👥👥 Students discuss the questions in pairs or small groups. Encourage them to use persuasive techniques from Exercise 5 and 6 in their discussion. After a few minutes, open up the discussion to include the whole class.

> **Answers will vary.**

CRITICAL THINKING

👥👥👥 Go through the task with the class. Elicit how the task is similar to or different from the discussion in Listening 2. (It is similar in that both are chaired discussions about saving energy; it is different in that Listening 2 was about an office while the speaking task is about a college/university.)

Identifying pros and cons when making a decision

👥👥👥 Elicit from the class what *pros* and *cons* are, then tell students to read the information in the book to check their ideas.

ANALYZE

1 👥 Students work in pairs to decide if the statements are pros or cons of removing a photocopier. Check answers with the class.

> **Answers**
> 1 P 2 P 3 C 4 C 5 P

EVALUATE

2 👥 Students discuss the questions in pairs. After a few minutes, open up the discussion to include the whole class.

Answers

1 Discussing pros and cons can help you understand possible consequences of an action.
2 You could choose the course of action with the most pros and the fewest cons from the list.

APPLY

3, 4 👥 Students work in pairs to complete the tables for their idea. You could encourage them to think of creative or unusual ideas rather than obvious ones. For the second table, make sure they know not to simply write the reverse of what they wrote for Exercise 3, but to come up with new pros and cons for not using the idea.

5, 6 👤👥 👥 Students work in their pairs to answer the questions. After a few minutes, put them together with another pair to discuss their ideas. Ask some students to feed back to the class on whether the other pair agreed with their conclusion.

Answers will vary.

SPEAKING

PREPARATION FOR SPEAKING

Asking for input, summarizing and keeping a discussion moving

👥 Elicit from the class another name for a chairperson of a meeting (chair) and what that person is expected to do during a meeting. Students look at the information in the book to check their ideas.

1 👤👥 Students work alone to match the sentences with the functions. They check in pairs and feed back to the class.

Answers

1 b 2 a 3 a 4 c 5 c 6 b

2, 3 🔊 8.5 👤👥 Students work alone to complete the dialogue. Play the recording for students to check their answers. They check in pairs and feed back to the class.

Answers

1 So, to summarize
2 Does anyone have anything to say
3 Sorry, but that's not really what we're

Using a neutral tone of voice

👥 Students close their books. Elicit from the class what a neutral tone of voice is and why it could be useful in a discussion. You could also elicit what it means if somebody's tone of voice sounds challenging. (Suggested answer: It sounds as if they disagree with you and don't really respect your opinion.) Students then look at the information in the box to compare it with their ideas.

4 🔊 8.6 👤👥 Play the first two examples for the class to make sure everyone can hear the difference between a neutral and challenging tone of voice. Then play the rest of the recording for students to complete the exercise. They check in pairs and feed back to the class.

Answers

3 C 4 N 5 N 6 C 7 C 8 N

5 👥 Students work in pairs to practise saying the sentences using a neutral or challenging tone of voice. You could ask some volunteers to say a sentence to the class, to see if the other students in the group can guess what tone of voice they are using.

Being firm but polite

👥 Students close their books. Elicit from the class why a chairperson sometimes needs to be firm but polite, and some phrases to make a firm request sound more polite. Students then read the information in the box to compare it with their ideas.

6 👤👥 Go through the examples in the box with the class. Tell students to underline all the differences between the direct and the polite versions of the sentences. Draw attention to the use of the -ing form after the phrase Would you mind … . Students then work in pairs to make the sentences more polite. When they are ready, elicit a range of answers from the class.

Suggested answers

1 Could you please wait until I've finished speaking?
2 Would you mind explaining what you mean?
3 That isn't really what we're talking about.
4 Sorry, but would you mind waiting until Tom finishes speaking?
5 Could you please repeat that?
6 Please could you save that for later in the discussion? We need to move on now.

SPEAKING TASK

👥 Point out that this is the same task that students prepared for in the Critical thinking section. Tell students to look at the Task checklist after Exercise 5, so that they know what is expected of them. Elicit from the class where they can find useful language for this type of speaking. (The Preparation for speaking section has useful language for all the points on the checklist as does Listening 2 and Exercises 5 and 6.) Divide the class into groups and make sure each student knows which point in the meeting they will chair. Note that points 1, 2, and 3 can all end with short summaries, while point 4 includes an overall summary of the whole meeting. If your class is not in a university or college, you could adapt the task to make it about the building you are in now, or any other building that all the students know well. Alternatively, you could get the students to imagine that they are in a university or college.

PREPARE

1, 2 👥 Students work in their groups to prepare for their meeting. At this stage, they are not role-playing the meeting, but rather brainstorming a list of ideas to save energy.

3, 4 👤 Students work alone to plan what points they will make in the discussion. Ideally, they should have at least one point to make for each item on the agenda. They make notes of digressions to look out for during their agenda point and useful language that they can use when they are chairing their part of the meeting.

PRACTISE

5 👥 Students work in their groups to role-play the meeting. You could set a limit of around five minutes per agenda item in order to make sure each student has a fair chance to act as chairperson. Monitor carefully while students are speaking to make notes of the good and bad examples of language that you hear. Pay particular attention to the phrases and structures students use from this unit. Ask volunteers from each group to report back on their conclusions at the end of the role-play. Afterwards, give and elicit feedback on the language used during the role-play.

TASK CHECKLIST / OBJECTIVES REVIEW

👥 Students complete the checklists in pairs and then report back to the class. Where they feel they need extra practice, discuss with the class how they can get this. You can also feed back individually to them on how well they are able to do the things in the table, and where they need extra practice.

WORDLIST

👥 Students work in pairs to explain the words in the list to a partner. Afterwards, ask volunteers to explain each word to the class.

REVIEW TEST

See page 111 for the photocopiable Review test for this unit and Teaching tips, page 90 for ideas about when and how to administer the Review test.

ADDITIONAL SPEAKING TASK

See page 124 for an additional speaking task related to this unit.

Write the title of the discussion on the board, and decide with students whether it should be about their city or country. Brainstorm a few initial ideas with the class and write them on the board. If students don't seem to know much about their own city/country, they could invent ideas for an imaginary place instead. Give each student a photocopy of the model language on page 124. Divide the class into small groups and allocate roles for the items on the agenda to each person. Students work alone to make notes and prepare for the meeting. They then hold the meeting, making sure they know to manage their own agenda item. At the end of the exercise, ask volunteers form each group to report back on their ideas to the class.

RESEARCH PROJECT

Write a blog about saving energy

Ask students research different ways energy is wasted (e.g. by not turning off lights). Then ask them to answer the following questions: 'How is my learning environment wasting energy?' and 'What can I do to help reduce this?'. Use online tools to list the problems and to come up with solutions.

Students each create a week-long blog in which they record what they have done to save energy every day. Students could follow each other's blogs and vote for the best energy-saving learner at the end of the week.

9 ART AND DESIGN

Learning objectives

👥👥👥 Go through the learning objectives with the class to make sure everyone understands what they can expect to achieve in this unit. Point out that students will have a chance to review these objectives again at the end of the unit.

Lead-in

👥👥👥 Before the lesson, search the internet for images of works of art. Use search terms such as *painting*, *modern art*, or *sculpture*. Print out a range of images and stick them up around the classroom. Keep a record of where you found each picture, so that you can tell students who the artist is, if they want to know.

Tell students to walk around the classroom and look at the pictures as if they were in a gallery. When everybody has had a chance to look at the pictures, ask volunteers to say which images they liked best, and explain why they liked them. As a follow-up, you could hold a class vote to decide on their favourite picture.

UNLOCK YOUR KNOWLEDGE

👥👥 👥👥👥 Check that everyone understands what a *sculpture* is, using the photograph as a reference. Students then discuss the questions in pairs or small groups. After a few minutes, open up the discussion to include the whole class.

> Answers will vary.

WATCH AND LISTEN

Video script

SCULPTURE

▶ At one of the busiest road junctions in Mexico City stands a giant yellow sculpture. It is called El Caballito and it is the work of Mexican artist Sebastián.

When Sebastián was a child, he collected crystals. The crystals inspired him to make sculptures using basic geometric shapes and bold, bright colours. He uses geometry and colour to express human feelings and emotions. Some of his sculptures are small and easy to display in galleries. Others are large and require more space.

Sebastián is travelling to a mine near his childhood home in Chihuahua, Mexico. Recently, the miners made an amazing discovery. Today, Sebastián is going underground to see it with his own eyes. Three

hundred metres underground, nature has created amazing, natural sculptures. Giant crystals – the biggest ever discovered – grow up from the floor towards the ceiling. Some of them are 15 metres long. The crystals formed thousands of years ago when the cave was filled with mineral-rich water. A volcano heated the water to about 58 degrees centigrade – perfect for growing crystals.

Sebastián has never seen anything like it – he is deeply impressed with these sculptures created by nature. The sculptor cannot stay in the cave for long because of the intense heat, but he has remained long enough to find inspiration for his next great work of art.

Sebastián is now designing a sculpture that will be as tall as a 12-storey building. When he has completed the design the construction of the sculpture can begin. Like El Caballito, this new work will stand at a major road junction in Mexico City. This area of the city is very flat, so the sculpture will be visible from a long way away.

Some of the pieces of the sculpture weigh two tonnes. Each piece must be lifted with a crane and carefully joined to the other pieces of the sculpture. It takes a huge team of people to construct a sculpture of this size. Like the giant crystals, Sebastián's sculpture slowly rises from the earth. Inspired by nature, the sculptor's work is truly amazing.

PREPARING TO WATCH

USING YOUR KNOWLEDGE TO PREDICT CONTENT

1 👥👥👥 Check that everyone understands what a *sculptor* is. (An artist who creates sculptures.) Students work in groups to discuss the questions. After a few minutes, ask volunteers from each group to report back to the class.

> Answers will vary.

UNDERSTANDING KEY VOCABULARY

2 👤 👥👥 Students work alone to match the sentence halves. They check in pairs and feed back to the class.

> **Answers**
> 1 f 2 d 3 e 4 b 5 c 6 a

Background note

- A *geometric* shape is any shape that can be described mathematically, in terms of straight lines, angles and curves. Examples include triangles, rectangles, circles, ellipses, semicircles, etc.
- A *regular* shape is one whose sides are all equal in length, and whose angles are all identical. Examples include equilateral triangles, squares, hexagons, etc.

Optional activity

Ask volunteers to draw three shapes on the board:

- a regular geometric shape,
- a non-regular geometric shape,
- a non-geometric shape.

Encourage the other students to give advice to the students who are drawing the shapes. Use the following questions to check students' understanding of the other key words in Exercise 2.

- What is the connection between *crystals* and *mines*? (Crystals often grow underground, so they are likely to be found in mines.)
- Where do artists get their *inspiration* to paint? (From nature, from their emotions, from their experiences, etc.)
- What is the opposite of an *intense* or *bold* colour? (A *pale* or *faint* colour.)
- What are some examples of different types of *junctions*? (A T-junction, a crossroads, a roundabout, etc.)

3 Students work in pairs to describe the photographs using the key words from Exercise 2. Check answers with the class.

| Answers will vary.

WHILE WATCHING

UNDERSTANDING MAIN IDEAS

4 Check that everyone understands all the words in the sentences, especially *inspired* and *huge*. Play the video for students to complete the sentences. Afterwards, they check in pairs and feed back to the class.

Answers

1 b 2 c 3 b 4 c

Background note

The sculptor *Sebastián* has produced over 200 monumental sculptures around the world. His most famous sculpture, *Cabeza de Caballo* (the Horse's Head), in the centre of Mexico City, is commonly known as "*El Caballito*" (the Little Horse).

LISTENING FOR KEY INFORMATION

5 Students work in pairs to try to remember the information from the fact file. You may need to check everyone understands the meaning of *noticeable* (easy to see). Play the video for them to check their answers and to complete the fact file. Afterwards, they compare answers again in pairs and feed back to the class.

Answers

1 Crystals and geometric shapes.
2 Human feelings and emotions.
3 In galleries and in public spaces.
4 He is inspired to make a new sculpture.
5 A major road junction in Mexico City.
6 It will be very large and on flat ground so it will be visible from a long way away.

DISCUSSION

6 Students work in pairs to discuss the questions. After a few minutes, open up the discussion to include the whole class.

| Answers will vary.

LISTENING 1

PREPARING TO LISTEN

UNDERSTANDING KEY VOCABULARY

1 Students work alone to match the words and definitions. They check in pairs and feed back to the class.

Answers

1 b 2 d 3 a 4 c 5 h 6 e 7 g 8 f

Language note

Note that the word *criticism* has two meanings. The first meaning, as explained in Exercise 1, is a form of negative feedback. The verb *criticize* normally has this negative meaning. The second meaning is that *criticism* is a form of analysis, whether positive or negative, typically conducted by an expert. An *art critic* is one such expert.

Optional activity

Students work in pairs to write a paragraph using all eight words from Exercise 1, using dictionaries if necessary. When they are ready, ask volunteers to read their paragraphs to the class.

Possible answer

There has been a lot of *criticism* of *street art* recently. Some people claim it is just *graffiti*, a type of *vandalism*. However, others have argued that it is an important form of *self-expression* and *creativity*. They say that the best street artists have a good understanding of *colour schemes* and artistic *composition*.

PREDICTING CONTENT USING VISUALS

2 👥 Students work in pairs to discuss the questions about the picture. After a few minutes, open up the discussion to include the whole class.

> **Answers will vary.**

3 👤👥 Students try to predict which person expressed each opinion about the painting. They check in pairs and feed back to the class. When you discuss the answers with the class, ask students to justify their answers but avoid confirming or rejecting their predictions, as these will be answered in the next task.

> **Answers**
> See Exercise 4.

WHILE LISTENING

LISTENING FOR GIST

4 ◀)) 9.1 👤👥 Play the recording for students to check their predictions from Exercise 3. Afterwards, they check in pairs and feed back to the class.

> **Answers**
> 1 c 2 a 3 e 4 b 5 d

Language note

Note that several of the speakers refer to the artist as *they*, meaning *he or she*, because it is not known if the artist is male or female. This usage is very common in spoken English, but some people consider it unacceptable in formal written English, where a structure using *he/she* is often preferred.

LISTENING FOR OPINION

5 ◀)) 9.1 👥 Students work in pairs to try to remember which speaker made each statement. Then play the recording again for them to check their ideas. They check in pairs, and feed back to the class.

> **Answers**
> b 2 c 1 d 2 e 4 f 1 g 5 h 5 i 4 j 3

POST LISTENING

MAKING INFERENCES

Inferring opinions

👥👥 Students close their books. Elicit from the class why somebody might conceal their true opinion on something, what *inferring opinions* means and how it might be possible to *infer* (/ ɪnˈfɜː/) somebody's hidden opinion. Tell students to read the information in the box to compare it with their ideas.

6 👥 Students discuss the questions in pairs. When they are ready, discuss the answers with the class.

> **Answers**
> 1 creative, the artist, piece of art, artistic, expressive, artwork
> 2 graffiti, our illegal painter, piece of vandalism
> 3 The Police officer; The Police officer's personal opinion differs from his professional view. The host should be neutral, but seems to dislike the painting.

PRONUNCIATION FOR LISTENING

Stress in word families

7 ◀)) 9.2 👤👥 Go through the examples of the words with stressed syllables with the class. Then play the recording for students to underline the stressed syllables in the rest of the words. They check in pairs and feed back. For number 7, point out that *permit* is used as a noun (document giving permission). When it is used as a verb, meaning *to allow*, the stress is on the second syllable: a <u>per</u>mit (noun) / to per<u>mit</u> (verb).

> **Answers**
> 3 com<u>mu</u>nicate, communi<u>ca</u>tion
> 4 cre<u>ate</u>, cre<u>a</u>tion
> 5 ex<u>hib</u>it, exhi<u>bi</u>tion
> 6 recom<u>mend</u>, recommen<u>da</u>tion
> 7 <u>per</u>mit, per<u>mit</u>ted
> 8 <u>art</u>ist, <u>art</u>istic

8 👥 Students work in pairs to practise pronouncing the word pairs with the correct stress.

DISCUSSION

9 👥 👥👥 Students work in pairs to discuss the questions. After a few minutes, open up the discussion to include the whole class.

| Answers will vary.

👁 LANGUAGE DEVELOPMENT

EXPRESSING CONTRASTING OPINIONS

Expressing contrasting opinions

👥👥👥 Tell students to close their books. Write the example sentence from the box on the board, with the bolded words underlined. Elicit from the class the technique used in the sentence to contrast the opinions. Then tell students to look at the information in the box to compare it with their ideas.

1 👥👥👥 Briefly discuss the questions with the class.

| Answers
|
| 1 The speaker thinks it's a piece of art. 2 *This looks like* 3 *but in fact*

2 👤 👥👥 Students work alone to complete the table. They check in pairs, and feed back to the class. When you go through the answers with the class, make sure everyone fully understands all of the phrases.

| Answers

introducing a statement	expressing a contrasting opinion
Many people think that We take it for granted that It seems as if It looks like Some people say It may seem	but in fact In reality, The fact of the matter is but actually, However, The truth of the matter is

Language note

If you *take something for granted*, you don't think about it and assume it will always be there. For example, teenagers often take their parents for granted, and only become aware of how much they did for them when they leave home.

3 👤 👥👥 Students work alone to rewrite the sentences. They check in pairs and feed back to the class.

| Answers
|
| 1 It may seem that a lot of money is spent on public art, but in fact only 0.5% of public money is spent on art.
| 2 Many people think that public art has no long-term cost. However, cleaning and maintenance need to be considered.
| 3 It seems like the new sculpture is very popular, but actually a thousand people signed a petition to have it removed.
| 4 It looks like the government wasted a lot of money on the sculpture. The fact of the matter is that it was donated to the city.

ACADEMIC VOCABULARY RELATED TO ART

4 👤 👥👥 Students work alone to match the words with the definitions. They check in pairs and feed back to the class. You may need to check the pronunciation of *appreciate* /əˈpriːʃieɪt/ and *interpret* /ɪnˈtɜprɪt/.

| Answers
|
| 1 e 2 a 3 i 4 c 5 g 6 h 7 d 8 f 9 j 10 b

Language note

The verb *appreciate* has three meanings, as shown by these examples:
- *Thanks for your help, I really appreciate it.* (I value it.)
- *I appreciate that the budget is tight, but …* (I understand it, I am aware of it.)
- *The value of my investments has appreciated significantly.* (Increased in terms of how much they are worth.)

Optional activity

👥👥👥 Elicit from the class the nouns that derive from the ten verbs in the previous exercise. Students can use a dictionary if necessary.

| Answers
|
| 1 appreciation 2 display 3 interpretation 4 rejection
| 5 removal 6 analysis 7 comment/commentary 8 focus
| 9 restoration 10 revelation

5 👤 👥👥 Students work alone to circle the verbs. They check in pairs and feed back to the class.

| Answers
|
| 1 appreciate 2 analyze 3 comment 4 display 5 focus
| 6 interpret 7 reject 8 remove

Optional activity

Students work in pairs to discuss who might have said each sentence in Exercise 5 and where they might have said it. When they are ready, elicit answers from the class.

Suggested answers

Sentences 1, 3 and 6 might have been spoken by an art critic commenting on paintings in a gallery.
Sentences 2 and 7 might have been spoken by an art critic commenting on a piece of street art.
Sentence 4 was probably spoken by the owner of an art gallery.
Sentences 5 and 8 might have been spoken by a police officer commenting on a piece of street art/ graffiti.

LISTENING 2

PREPARING TO LISTEN

USING YOUR KNOWLEDGE

1 👥 Students work in pairs to discuss the questions. After a few minutes, open up the discussion to include the whole class.

| Answers will vary.

WHILE LISTENING

LISTENING FOR MAIN IDEAS

2 (◀) 9.3 👤👥 Tell students to read through the points to check they understand them. You could ask them to decide which of the points are generally in favour of selling the sculpture (1, 5 and 7) and which are generally in favour of keeping it (2, 3, 4, 6 and 8). Play the recording for students to check which points are mentioned. They check answers in pairs and feed back to the class.

Answers

1, 3, 5, 6, 8

3, 4 (◀) 9.3 👥 Students work in pairs to try to remember as much as possible about the missing information in the notes. Point out that they should make very brief notes, not write full sentences. Play the recording again for students to complete the notes. They check in pairs again and feed back to the class.

Answers

1 Decision 1: Find out what the sculpture is worth.
2 Response 2.2: We can probably find something that will be popular enough.
3 Decision 2: To put together a proposal.
4 Response 3.1: The location is the problem.
5 Decision 3: Do more research on locations and cost.
6 Response 4.1: A public sports centre reflects the needs of people more.
7 Decision 4: Need to find out if selling the sculpture is legal.

POST LISTENING

Thinking about fact and opinion

👥 Students close their books. Elicit from the class the difference between *facts* and *opinions*, and the role of each of them in a debate. Then tell students to read the information in the box and compare it with their ideas.

5 👤👥 Students work alone to decide if the points are facts or opinions. They check in pairs and feed back to the class.

Answers

1 F 2 O 3 F 4 F 5 O 6 O 7 F 8 O

6 👥 Students work in pairs to do the exercise. You may need to go through the first question with the class as an example to make sure everyone understands what to do. Students then work in pairs to form positive and negative opinions based on the information. When they have finished, elicit a range of ideas from the class.

Possible answers:

1 A sports centre will be a great use of public money./ We may not have the money to build a sports centre.
2 Moving the sculpture will bring tourists to the shopping centre. / £10,000 is too much to spend on moving the sculpture to the shopping centre.
3 A national art collector will be able to look after the sculpture very well. / We need to keep the sculpture so the public can enjoy it.
4 Hiring a security guard would keep the sculpture safe from vandals and graffiti artists. / It would be a waste of money to hire a security guard to watch the sculpture at night.

DISCUSSION

7 Students work in pairs or small groups to discuss the questions. Encourage them to use a mixture of facts and opinions in their discussions. After a few minutes, open up the discussion to include the whole class.

| Answers will vary.

CRITICAL THINKING

Go through the task with the class. Tell students to read the box to find ways in which it is similar to and different from the debate in Listening 2. (The topic is very similar, although the speaking task will be about the place where students live. Another small difference is that the debate in Listening 2 was specifically about a sculpture, whereas the speaking task is about a piece of public art, which could be anything.) If there isn't any public art near where the students live, you can still try to make the discussion as real as possible by getting the class to imagine exactly what the art is and where it might be located in their town/city.

ANALYZE

Debate statements and responses

Students close their books. Elicit from the class the difference between a *statement* and a *response* in a debate. Students then look at the information in the box to compare it with their ideas.

1 Students work alone to complete the matching exercise. They check in pairs and feed back to the class.

| Answers
| 1 a 2 b 3 d 4 c

2 Students work in pairs to rewrite the sentences. Check answers with the class.

| Answers
| 1 I don't think we should spend money on public art for our college campus.
| 2 But public art has been found to increase positivity.
| 3 The money should probably be spent on better education facilities.
| 4 Look further at the costs and benefits of public art on campus.

CREATE

3, 4 Go through the instructions with the class. Point out that students write a response in each box, so they need a total of four responses. Encourage them to use phrases from Exercises 1 and 2 in the sentences they write. Students work in pairs to plan and write their sentences.

5 In the same pairs, students plan and write some final decisions for statements A and B, using the phrases from Exercises 1 and 2.

6 Each pair works with another pair to compare and discuss their responses and decisions. Afterwards, ask volunteers to share any interesting differences with the class.

| Answers will vary.

SPEAKING

PREPARATION FOR SPEAKING

1 Go through the instructions and the example with the class, to make sure students know what to do. They then work in pairs to practise saying the sentences using a range of words and expressions from the box.

| Answers will vary.

2 Students work in pairs. You may want to do an example sentence with the class, to show that there are two ways of combining the opinions. Students then work in pairs to contrast the opinions using a range of structures from Exercise 1. When they have finished, ask volunteers to present some of their sentences to the class.

| Answers will vary.

Language for hedging

Tell students to read the information in the box and the examples to find out what *hedging* is. Elicit from the class what techniques are used in the examples.

Suggested answer

The first four examples all suggest that the statement is the speaker's personal opinion and acknowledge that this opinion may be wrong. In the next four examples, the speaker is careful not to disagree with the other person, before presenting an alternative to their point of view. Note that the comments on the other person's opinion are all positive. (*You could say that*, *that's true*, etc.)

> ### Language note
>
> The term *hedging* comes from an idiomatic expression, *to hedge your bets*, which means planning for a range of outcomes. If one of your plans fails, you still have other options available. Hedging is therefore a way of reducing the risk of failure in an activity.

3 Students work in pairs to make the opinions and answers more polite by using hedging techniques. Make sure students know to swap roles after each opinion. Afterwards, elicit a range of answers from the class.

> **Answers will vary.**

PRONUNCIATION FOR SPEAKING

Stress in hedging language

Tell students to look at the information in the Pronunciation focus box. Draw their attention to the example sentence, and ask some volunteers to try to say the phrase with the correct pronunication.

4, 5 ◀) 9.4 Students work in pairs to predict which words will be stressed in Exercise 4. Play the recording for them to check their ideas. Students then practise pronouncing the phrases in pairs.

> ### Answers
>
> 2 *I'm* not an expert, but ...
> 3 All *I* know is ...
> 4 For *me*, ...
> 5 You *could* say that, however *actually* ...
> 6 That's true *in part*, but *I* think ...
> 7 You *may* be right, but *I* wonder if ...
> 8 *I see* what you're saying, but *maybe* ...

> ### Optional activity
>
> Students work in pairs to repeat Exercise 3 without looking back at Exercises 4 and 5, paying particular attention to the pronunciation of the hedging phrases.

Restating somebody's point

Students close their books. Elicit from the class two reasons why you might need to restate somebody's point in a debate. Then tell students to read the information box to compare it with their ideas.

6 Students work alone to decide if the statements are clarifications or arguments. They check in pairs and feed back to the class.

> ### Answers
>
> 1 C 2 A 3 A 4 C

7 Students work in pairs and take turns making and restating the points. Encourage them to extend their dialogues and use the phrases from Exercise 4 and 6 several times in each discussion. Afterwards, you could ask some volunteers to act out part of their discussions for the class.

> **Answers will vary.**

> ### Optional activity
>
> Write the following statements on the board:
> - Design is more important than art – designers make useful things, while artists just make pretty things.
> - These days, the design of technology products is more important than the technology itself.
> - The main purpose of design is to make older products unfashionable so we spend more money on new ones.
>
> Students work in small groups to debate the three statements, using all the techniques from the Preparation for speaking section to help them.

SPEAKING TASK

Point out that this is the same task that students prepared for in the Critical thinking section. Tell students to look at the Task checklist after Exercise 6, so that they know what is expected of them. Elicit from the class where they can find useful language for this type of debate. (The Preparation for speaking section has useful language for all the points on the checklist.)

PREPARE

1 👥👥👥 Divide the class into groups. The ideal group size is three, but smaller or larger groups are also possible. Students work together to discuss the positive and negative aspects of keeping the sculpture. Discuss with the class briefly to find out which groups are in favour of the sculpture being sold, and which groups are against it. Ideally, there should be a good balance between the two sides, so you may need to ask some groups to switch sides for the purposes of the debate.

PRACTISE

2, 3, 4, 5 👥👥👥 Students work in their groups to plan and practise what they will say in the debate. Make sure they know to include the language and techniques from this unit in their points.

DISCUSS

6 👥👥👥 Put the students into new groups of three. Ideally, each new group should contain at least one person from each side of the debate. Make sure everyone knows how and why to keep notes in the table. Point out that they will need to make joint decisions during the debate. You may want to set a time limit for the debates, e.g. ten minutes. Monitor carefully while students are speaking to make notes of the good and bad examples of language that you hear. Pay particular attention to the phrases and structures students use from this unit. Ask volunteers from each group to report back on their decisions from the meeting. Afterwards, give and elicit feedback on the language used during the debate.)

TASK CHECKLIST / OBJECTIVES REVIEW

👥👥 Students complete the checklists in pairs and then report back to the class. Where they feel they need extra practice, discuss with the class how they can get this. You can also feed back individually to them on how well they are able to do the things in the table, and where they need extra practice.

WORDLIST

👥👥 Students work in pairs to explain the words in the list to a partner. Afterwards, ask volunteers to explain each word to the class.

REVIEW TEST

See page 113 for the photocopiable Review test for this unit and Teaching tips, page 90 for ideas about when and how to administer the Review test.

ADDITIONAL SPEAKING TASK

See page 125 for an additional speaking task related to this unit.

Explain the situation tin the speaking task to the class. Elicit some possible arguments in favour of and against the exhibition, e.g. it may inspire the students, attract visitors and raise the university/college's profile. However, it may also be expensive to organize, especially to ensure there is adequate security for the works of art. Give each student a photocopy of the model language on page 125. Divide the class into groups of three and tell them to decide quickly whether they are for or against the exhibition. If necessary, you may need to tell some groups to change sides, in order to get a good for/against balance in the debate. Students work in their groups to plan and practise their arguments. Put them into new groups of three, making sure each new group contains at least one person in favour of and one person against the exhibition. Students debate the issue in their groups. At the end of the exercise, ask volunteers to report back on the outcome of their debates to the class.

RESEARCH PROJECT

Create a TV programme discussing art and opinion

Divide the class into groups. Ask each group to search for pictures by a famous artist and to decide on one they all like. Tell them to write a brief critique of the pictures, noting down what their first impressions are, what feelings the art generates, who the artist was/is, their background, etc. Search 'how to critique artwork' for areas to focus on.

Each group's critique will then contribute to a script for an 'Art Critic' TV programme, which students will produce as a class. The resulting video can then be uploaded to a video-sharing website.

10 AGEING

Learning objectives

👥 Go through the learning objectives with the class to make sure everyone understands what they can expect to achieve in this unit. Point out that students will have a chance to review these objectives again at the end of the unit.

Lead-in

👥 Write the following discussion topic and questions on the board:

Some experts believe that the first person who will live to 200 years old is already alive now. How could this be possible? Would you like to be that person? Why / why not?

Students discuss the questions in small groups. After a few minutes, open up the discussion to include the whole class.

Suggested answers

Life expectancy has been increasing for centuries, and this increase has been accelerating recently. Researchers are making good progress in their fight against many diseases. They are also getting a better understanding of the ageing process and working out ways of slowing it down. It is currently possible for people to live to over 110 years old, so the expectation is that by the time today's babies are 110 years old, life expectancy will have further increased.

Background note

For an interesting introduction to this topic, search the internet for the phrase "live to 200 years old".

UNLOCK YOUR KNOWLEDGE

👥 👥 Students work in pairs or small groups to discuss the questions. After a few minutes, open up the discussion to include the whole class.

Answers will vary.

WATCH AND LISTEN

Video script

TAKING CARE OF THE FAMILY

▶ This is Ali. Like many children in Egypt, he works hard to support his ageing parents.

Cairo is one of the most densely populated cities in the world with an approximate population of seventeen million. Ali was sent to work in Cairo from his home in the south when he was just seven years old. He has worked at this bakery for 10 years now. Ali delivers bread to people. He is the only member of his family who works.

20% of the population in Cairo live in poverty. Families where older members find it hard to secure employment often rely on the younger relatives to provide income for food and household bills. It is often more cost-effective for shops and businesses to employ children. As a result, older generations can find themselves unemployed.

Starting at dawn, Ali works all day, earning up to six dollars. Keeping just one dollar for himself, he sends the rest back home to help his parents and younger brothers in his village. Ali works for up to 10 hours every day. It's gruelling work. He lives with a group of boys who also work every day in Cairo. Far away from home and missing their families, the boys have become good friends. They don't go to school but the money they send home may mean that their younger brothers and sisters can.

Ali hasn't seen his family for 10 months, but today is a holiday and he's returning to his village. 81% of all children working in Cairo are from rural areas, like Ali.

Everyone in the village is pleased to see him. His mother and father are thankful for the money he has sent home to provide for his family. They are unable to find work in their own village and would be unlikely to find work elsewhere. Although Ali is unable to go to school, the money means his younger brothers can attend and will therefore have a better chance of getting a good job when they are older. 13% of children in Egypt have never been to school.

For now, Ali and his family all enjoy the reunion and the little time they share together, as he will soon return to the bakery. But, unless the employment situation in Egypt changes, the question remains as to whether Ali and his brothers will experience the same economic problems as their parents when they grow older.

PREPARING TO WATCH

UNDERSTANDING KEY VOCABULARY

1 👤👥 Students work alone to read the paragraph and match the words with the definitions. They check in pairs and feed back to the class.

Answers

1 g 2 e 3 d 4 f 5 b 6 c 7 a 8 h

Answers

1 What is the population of Cairo?
2 How old was Ali when he was sent to work in Cairo?
3 What percentage of the population of Cairo lives in poverty?
4 How much does Ali earn a day? How much does he send to his family?
5 How many hours a day does Ali work? How many days a week does Ali work?
6 How long has it been since Ali has seen his family?
7 What percentage of children working in Cairo are from rural areas?
8 What percentage of Egyptian children have never received an education?

DISCUSSION

5 👥 👥👥 Students work in pairs or small groups to discuss the questions. After a few minutes, open up the discussion to include the whole class.

Answers will vary.

LISTENING 1

PREPARING TO LISTEN

USING YOUR KNOWLEDGE

1 👥👥 Students discuss the questions in groups. After a few minutes, open up the discussion to include the whole class.

Answers will vary.

UNDERSTANDING KEY VOCABULARY

2 👤👥 Students work alone to complete the sentences. They check in pairs and feed back to the class.

Answers

1 Retirement 2 luxuries 3 investments 4 consumer 5 finance 6 pension 7 property 8 Assets

---

Language note

The spelling of the word *ageing* is unusual. Unlike most verbs ending in -e, the verb to age keeps its -e when the -ing ending is added. However, the alternative spelling, *aging*, is also acceptable, especially in American English.

USING YOUR KNOWLEDGE TO PREDICT CONTENT

2 👥 Check that everyone understands the meanings of *urban* (related to cities) and *rural* (related to the countryside). Students discuss the questions in pairs. After a few minutes, open up the discussion to include the whole class.

Answers will vary.

WHILE WATCHING

UNDERSTANDING MAIN IDEAS

3 ▶️👤👥 Tell students to read through the statements and play the video for students to decide if they are true or false. They check answers in pairs and feed back to the class.

Answers

1 F 2 F 3 F 4 F

Background note

The population of Cairo includes almost seven million people within the city boundaries, and an additional 10 million people in the greater urban area.

LISTENING FOR KEY INFORMATION

4 ▶️👤👥 Students work in pairs to try to remember the questions for the answers in the exercise. Point out that they should take notes, and not try to write questions in full while watching. Play the video again. Students then work in pairs to make the complete questions. Go through the answers with the class.

WHILE LISTENING

LISTENING FOR GIST

3 (◀ 10.1) 👤👥 Check that everyone understands what a *podcast* is. (A video or audio recording posted onto a website or blog, typically giving advice or commentary.) Students then read through and check they understand all the subjects. Play the recording for students to tick the subjects that are mentioned. They check in pairs and feed back to the class.

> **Answers**
> 1, 3, 5, 6, 7

LISTENING FOR DETAIL

4 (◀ 10.1) 👥 Students work in pairs to try to complete the notes. You may need to check they understand what a *fraction* is. (A number expressed as one number divided by another, e.g. ½ (half), ¾ (three-quarters), etc.) Play the recording a second time for students to check and to complete the notes. They check again in pairs and feed back to the class.

> **Answers**
> 1 500 billion 2 240 billion 3 60 4 535 million 5 345 million 6 62 7 £400,000 8 2/3 (two-thirds) 9 more than 20%

> **Suggested answers**
> 1 meals in restaurants
> 2 we've worked hard enough to deserve it (morally)
> 3 look after children while their parents are away
> 4 There's no good reason why we shouldn't enjoy life.
> 5 We've fulfilled our obligations.

POST LISTENING

Understanding specific observations and generalizations

👥 Students close their books. Elicit from the class the difference between *specific observations* and *generalizations* and why it is useful to be able to distinguish between them. Tell students to read the information in the box to compare it with their ideas.

5 👤👥 Students work alone to decide if the statements are specific observations or generalizations. They check in pairs and feed back to the class.

> **Answers**
> 3 S 4 S 5 G 6 S 7 G 8 G

6 👤👥 Students work alone to complete the table. They check in pairs and feed back.

> **Answers**
>
> | specific observation | generalization |
> | --- | --- |
> | 1 | 2 |
> | 3 | 8 |
> | 4 | 7 |
> | 6 | 5 |

PRONUNCIATION FOR LISTENING

Elision and intrusion

👥 Tell students to read the information in the box to find the difference between *intrusion* and *elision*. When you check with the class, elicit or provide some examples of intrusion and elision for them.

Language note

Intrusion is used to make it easier to pronounce words together, most commonly when one word ends in a vowel sound and the next word starts with a vowel sound. The inserted sound appears to be joined to the beginning of the second word.

- When the first word ends with the sound /i/ or /ɪ/ (or a diphthong such as /ɪː/, /eɪ/, /aɪ/ or /ɔɪ/), there appears to be a /j/ inserted at the beginning of the next word, e.g. *we are* /wi jɑː/.
- When the first word ends with the sound /u/ or /ʊ/ (or a diphthong such as /ʊː/, /aʊ/ or /eʊ/), there appears to be a /w/ inserted at the beginning of the next word, e.g. *you are* /ju wɑː/.
- When the first word ends with any other vowel sound, there appears to be a /r/ inserted at the beginning of the next word, especially in British English, e.g. *wear out* /weə raʊt/. Note that this /r/ sound is usually present in the spelling, but not always (e.g. *China and* /tʃaɪnə rənd/). In American English, this /r/ sound is usually part of the normal pronunciation. Words like *wear* and *car* end in a voiced consonant sound, so we don't describe it as insertion.

Elision, where two words said together appear to lose a letter, also makes pronunciation easier.

- The most common form of elision is between the final /d/ from *and*, e.g. *you and me* /ju wən mi/.
- The sound /h/ is often elided from the beginning of grammatical words like *has* and *he*, e.g. *Has he gone?* /(h)əz (h)i gɒn?/
- Another common form is the elision of /t/ sounds from the middle of consonant clusters, e.g. *nex(t) year* /neks(t)jɪə/, *ac(t)s* /æk(t)s/, *don't know* /dəʊn(t) nəʊ/.
- Note that replacing one sound for another (e.g. /n/ instead of /ŋ/ in *-ing* words) is a form of substitution, not elision.

7, 8 🔊 **10.2** 👥 Students work in pairs to try to predict the pronunciation of the words in bold, looking at the two examples to help them. Play the recording for them to complete the table. Students then work in pairs again to practise saying the sentences with natural pronunciation.

Answers

3 /w/ 4 lost sound 5 /j/ 6 /w/ 7 /j/ 8 lost sound

DISCUSSION

9 👥👥👥 Students discuss the question in pairs or small groups. After a few minutes, open up the discussion to include the whole class.

Answers will vary.

⊙ LANGUAGE DEVELOPMENT

VERBS WITH INFINITIVES

Verbs followed by *to* + infinitive

👥👥👥 Students close their books. Write the two example sentences from the box on the board, with the bolded words underlined. Elicit from the class what the two underlined phrases have in common (they both contain the structure verb + *to*-infinitive) and how they are different (the second example has an object between the verb and *to*-infinitive). Elicit from the class a range of other verbs which follow the same two patterns. Then tell students to read the information in the box to compare it with their ideas.

1 👤👥👥 Students work alone to correct the sentences. They check in pairs and feed back to the class.

Answers

1 We always advise our daughters **to** live life to the full.
2 We want **to** encourage other people to retire early.
3 We **managed to** save enough money when we were working.
4 We would **not consent to going** into a retirement home.
5 We refuse **to** spend our retirement at home.
6 I won't force my children **to** take care of me.

2, 3 👥👥👥 Students work in pairs to rewrite the sentences. Make sure they know to use the structure verb + *to*-infinitive in their answers. They compare their ideas with another pair and then feed back to the class.

Answers

2 My wife didn't agree to the idea at first.
3 We will arrange to have our children taken care of.
4 We would never threaten to not leave our children any inheritance.

ACADEMIC VERBS FOR SUPPORT AND ASSISTANCE

4 🧍👥 Students work alone to match the pairs of words. They check in pairs and feed back to the class. Point out that the phrase *give* (oneself) *to* is idiomatic and not commonly used.

Answers

1 c 2 a 3 f 4 b 5 e 6 d 7 g 8 h

Answers

permission, devotion, contribution, assistance, cooperation, indication, participation

5 🧍👥 Students work alone to complete the sentences. They check in pairs and feed back to the class.

Answers

1 cooperate 2 permit 3 ensure 4 contribute 5 assist 6 indicate 7 devote 8 participate

LISTENING 2

PREPARING TO LISTEN

UNDERSTANDING KEY VOCABULARY

1 🧍👥 Students work alone to match the words and definitions. They check in pairs and feed back to the class.

Answers

1 a 2 i 3 g 4 b 5 f 6 e 7 d 8 h 9 c 10 j

USING YOUR KNOWLEDGE

2, 3 👥 Students discuss the questions in pairs, and then compare their ideas with another pair. After a few minutes, open up the discussion to include the whole class.

Answers will vary.

WHILE LISTENING

LISTENING FOR GIST

4 (◀) 10.3 🧍👥 Students read through the fact files and predict which country in the box the statistics relate to. Play the recording for students to check their predictions. They check in pairs and feed back to the class.

Answers

1 Japan 2 Egypt 3 Turkey

LISTENING FOR DETAIL

5 (◀) 10.3 👥 Students work in pairs to try to remember which topic was mentioned in the context of which country. Play the recording again for them to check their ideas. They check in pairs again and feed back to the class.

Answers

	Fahad, Egypt	Mika, Japan	Ahmet, Turkey
1 family support system for caring for the elderly	✓	✓	✓
2 the government's role in caring for the elderly	✓	✓	
3 caring for an elderly aunt in the home	✓		
4 the lifestyle of 20- and 30-year olds		✓	
5 changes in population size due to fertility rates	✓	✓	✓
6 the pros and cons of caring for an elderly person in the home			✓

POST LISTENING

6 👤👥 Students work alone to decide if the phrases in bold relate to a cause or effect. They check in pairs and feed back to the class.

Answers

1 E 2 C 3 E 4 C 5 E 6 E

DISCUSSION

7 👥👥👥 Students discuss the questions in pairs or small groups. Encourage them to use cause and effect phrases in their discussions. After a few minutes, open up the discussion to include the whole class.

Answers will vary.

CRITICAL THINKING

👥👥👥 Go through the task with the class. Elicit from the class why imaginary countries (A, B, C) are used instead of real countries in the task. (To focus students' attention on the data provided, rather than relying on any prior geographical knowledge.)

ANALYZE

Line graphs

👥👥👥 Tell students to read the information in the box and find two important things to look out for when analyzing a line graph. (Significant or unusual features; the main trends of data.)

1 👤👥👥 Students work alone to answer the questions. They check in pairs and feed back to the class.

Answers

1 The number of people aged 65 or older.
2 years   3 A and C; B   4 28%   5 20%   6 28%

EVALUATE

2 👥👥 Students work in pairs to match the statements to the countries. Check that everyone understands the meanings of the words *steadily* and *rapidly*. Check answers with the class.

Answers

1 A 2 C 3 B

3 👤👥👥 Students work alone to match the statements to the countries. They check in pairs and feed back to the class.

Answers

1 B 2 C 3 A 4 B 5 A 6 C

UNDERSTAND

4, 5 👥👥 Students work in pairs to answer the questions and complete the table.

Answers will vary.

Suggested answers

- Similarities: *both X and Y; also; in the same way; similarly;* etc.
- Differences: *while/whereas; on the other hand; in contrast;* etc.

6 👥👥👥 Students compare their answers with another pair and feed back to the class.

Answers will vary.

SPEAKING

PREPARATION FOR SPEAKING

REFERENCING DATA IN A PRESENTATION

1 👤👥 Students work alone to match the descriptions with the countries. They check in pairs and feed back to the class.

> **Answers**
>
> 1 Country B 2 Country A 3 Country B 4 Country B
> 5 Country A 6 Country B

2 👥 Students work in pairs to describe the other parts of the graphs. Encourage them to use the useful language from Exercise 1 as much as possible. When they are ready, ask volunteers to present their descriptions to the class.

> **Answers will vary.**

Explaining causes and effects

👥👥 Students close their books. Elicit from the class why it is important to explain causes and effects when describing graphs. Students then look at the information in the box to compare it with their ideas.

3 👤👥 Students work alone to match the sentence halves. They check in pairs and feed back to the class.

> **Answers**
>
> 1 c/e 2 c/e 3 a 4 b 5 d

4 👥 Students work in pairs to write sentences using the five expressions in the middle column. When students are ready, ask volunteers to present their sentences to the class.

Possible answers

People living longer can be traced back to improvements in medical care.
A population decrease was the result of people moving out of the country.
A population increase accounts for an increase in the number of over-65s.
The steady population was the result of the high number of over 65s.

Contrastive stress in comparisons

👥👥 Tell students to read the information in the box to find which words are usually stressed when making comparisons. (The numbers and the comparison word.) Elicit from the class some examples of comparison words. (*More*, *bigger*, *the same*, etc.)

5 🔊 10.4 👥 Students work in pairs to predict which words will be stressed in the sentences. Play the recording for students to check their predictions and to underline the stressed words. They check in pairs again and feed back to the class.

> **Answers**
>
> 1 Today, the over-65s make up <u>2.5%</u> of Country A's total population. This figure is <u>smaller than</u> the figure of <u>7%</u> for Country B.
> 2 The population of Country A will be <u>77 million</u> in 2050. This number is <u>much larger</u> than the figure of <u>1.4 million</u> for Country B.
> 3 By 2050 Country A's population will have risen to <u>1.78 million</u> people. The population for Country B <u>also</u> peaks in 2050 with <u>9.2 million</u> people.

6 👥 Students work in pairs to practise saying the sentences, paying particular attention to the contrastive stress.

Suggested answers

Turkey's population is nearly <u>80 million</u> today. If you look at the graph I've provided, you will see that more than <u>five</u> million people, or around <u>6.4%</u>, are over 65. This is only <u>slightly higher</u> than the number for <u>Egypt</u> and much <u>lower</u> than <u>Japan's 23%</u>. UN projections indicate that by <u>2050</u>, Turkey's population will reach <u>92</u> million and about <u>18</u> million people, or <u>20%</u> of the total, will be <u>over 65</u>. This is <u>higher</u> than the <u>16.8%</u> figure that we heard for <u>Egypt</u>, but much <u>lower</u> than <u>Japan's 38%</u>. So we can see that in the <u>long-term</u>, the <u>same</u> challenges lie ahead for <u>Turkey</u> as for <u>Egypt</u> and <u>Japan</u>. However, for <u>now</u>, the solution is for Turks to <u>continue</u> caring for the elderly at <u>home</u>.

SPEAKING TASK

Point out that this is the same task that students prepared for in the Critical thinking section. Tell students to look at the Task checklist after Exercise 6 so that they know what is expected of them. Elicit from the class where they can find useful language for this type of speaking. (All of the points were covered in the Preparation for speaking section; in addition, there was work on cause and effect language after Listening 2.) Divide the class into groups and assign one country to each group.

PREPARE

1, 2, 3, 4 In their groups, students work through the exercises. Monitor carefully to ensure that they understand all the additional information, and to help them plan and prepare their presentations.

PRACTISE

5, 6 Make sure each student has a chance to practise the presentation in their group. Students then form new groups and give their presentation. Monitor carefully while students are speaking to make notes of the good and bad examples of language that you hear. Pay particular attention to the phrases and structures students use from this unit. Afterwards, give and elicit feedback on the language used during the presentation.

TASK CHECKLIST / OBJECTIVES REVIEW

Students complete the checklists in pairs and then report back to the class. Where they feel they need extra practice, discuss with the class how they can get this. You can also feed back individually to them on how well they are able to do the things in the table, and where they need extra practice.

WORDLIST

Students work in pairs to explain the words in the list to a partner. Afterwards, ask volunteers to explain each word to the class.

REVIEW TEST

See page 115 for the photocopiable Review test for this unit and Teaching tips, page 90 for ideas about when and how to administer the Review test.

ADDITIONAL SPEAKING TASK

See page 126 for an additional speaking task related to this unit. Before you start the task, elicit from the class some types of employment (full-time, part-time, voluntary work, etc.) and some factors that might affect how many people over 60 are in these types of employment; retirement age (the age at which people receive a state pension), life expectancy, general population growth, attitudes to work (including voluntary work), availability of suitable jobs, etc. Give each student a photocopy of the model language on page 126. Divide the class into groups of about four students. Each group should choose one line on the graph to analyze and describe, speculating on additional causes and effects that relate to the line as well as those in the fact file. Allow plenty of time for them to prepare and practise their presentations. Put them into new groups to deliver their presentations to other students. As a follow-up, ask volunteers from each group to report back on similarities and differences between their presentations.

RESEARCH PROJECT

Create an 'infographic' showing the effects of an ageing population

Divide the class into groups and explain that each group will be responsible for researching one of the effects an ageing population can have on a country. These could include issues related to work, retirement, healthcare, taxation, education and the economy. Each group researches one of these areas, using online tools to share ideas and research.

Using a slideshow app or infographics software (search 'infographics'), each group designs infographics to show and share the information they have found with the rest of the class.

The *Review tests* are designed to be used after the students have completed each unit of the Student's book. Each *Review test* checks students' knowledge of the key language areas and practices the listening skills from the unit. The *Review tests* take around 50 minutes to complete but you may wish to adjust this time depending on your class or how much of the Student's book unit you covered.

Review tests can be given as homework as general revision. *Review test* audio is accessed from the Cambridge LMS. Use the *Additional speaking tasks* at the end of the Teacher's Book or in the Online Workbook to test your students' speaking skills. Photocopy one test for each student. Students should do the tests on their own. You can check the answers by giving students their peers' papers to mark or correct the papers yourself. Keep a record of the results to help monitor individual student progress.

REVIEW TEST 1 ANSWERS

1 China
Much too slowly: 4%
A bit too slowly: 13%
About right/don't know: 11%
A bit too quickly: 49%
Much too quickly: 23%

Turkey
Much too slowly: 28%
A bit too slowly: 43%
About right/don't know: 14%
A bit too quickly: 12%
Much too quickly: 3%

2 1 b 2 a 3 b 4 b 5 c
3 1 c 2 a 3 e 4 b 5 d
4

	1↓								
2	A	G	R	I	C	U	L	T	U	R	E
3		P	U	R	C	H	A	S	E
4		P	R	O	C	E	S	S	I	N	G
5		I	M	P	O	R	T	E	D
6	C	O	N	S	U	M	E	R	S

5 1 Food is often transported by aeroplane.
2 Farmers in poor countries should be paid more for the food that they produce.
3 Agricultural products from my country are sold in shops all over the world.
4 Your carbon footprint can be reduced if you eat local foods.
5 These vegetables weren't imported-they're from this country.

REVIEW TEST AUDIOSCRIPTS 1

🔊 **1.1**

These pie charts show attitudes to globalization in two different countries. The one on the left is for China, where globalization seems to be unpopular, and the one on the right is for Turkey, where people seem to be very positive about it.

Let's start with China. As you can see, 23% of Chinese believe that globalization is happening much too quickly. A further 49% think it's a bit too quick. Only 4% of people in China feel that globalization is happening much too slowly and 13% said it was a bit too slow, giving a total of only 17% who want it to happen faster. That leaves 11% of Chinese who said that the pace of globalization was about right, as well those who said they didn't know. This data is surprising because we usually think of China as one of the countries that has benefitted most from globalization. However, it does cause many changes to people's lifestyles, so some people perhaps just want this to slow down a bit.

Now let's turn to Turkey, where attitudes to globalization are very different. In Turkey, 28% of the population said it was happening much too slowly and a further 43% said it was happening a bit too slowly. Only 3% of people in Turkey felt that globalization was happening much too quickly, and 12% felt that it was a bit too quickly. 14% of people either didn't know or said that the pace of globalization was about right; slightly more than in China. I would love to know why so many people in Turkey feel positive about globalization – maybe people there welcome change much more than in most other countries. The only other country …

🔊 **1.2**

Presenter: Hello, and welcome to Culture Zone. Today we're talking about the impact of globalization on culture. I'm joined by Dr Amy Martin, an expert on the topic. Dr Martin, should we be worried about globalization?

Dr Martin: Perhaps not worried, but we do need to be aware of its problems. We need to ask if the cultural changes resulting from globalization have been positive or negative. The most obvious change in recent decades is the increasing popularity of American culture. American films, music and clothes can now be found all over the world and a lot of people feel uncomfortable with this.

P: Because it means they have less contact with their own culture?

M: Possibly, although Americanization usually adds to, rather than replaces, local cultures. Actually, if you look under the surface, you'll see that most people around the world spend at least 50% of their time interacting with their own culture, through locally-made TV programmes, books and newspapers, and so on. So there's only a small percentage of any culture that's truly international, but that's often the part that's most visible.

P: I see. And when you say international, do you mean English-speaking?

M: Not at all. In fact, I think we're going to see a lot more non-English international music and films in future. International used to mean American because that was where the film and music industries were based. But nowadays, thanks to the internet, we'll start seeing much more work from a wider range of countries. If you think about it, true globalization, in the sense of cultural works coming from around the world, is only just beginning. And I, for one, am really excited about it.

P: Yes, I see what you mean. Dr. Martin, do you think …

REVIEW TEST 2 ANSWERS

1 1 advertising 2 accounting 3 bank 4 Geology
  5 software

2 1F 2A 3A 4H 5F

3 1C 2U 3U 4C 5C

4 1b 2a 3a 4b 5a

5 1 theoretical 2 in-depth 3 exhausted 4 complex
  5 weightless 6 acquire 7 career 8 apprentice
  9 specialist 10 vocational

6 1 Where would you like to study?
  2 Correct
  3 I'd rather you asked your teacher, not me.
  4 Correct
  5 Would you rather do a 3- or 4- year course?

REVIEW TEST AUDIOSCRIPTS 2

🔊 **2.1**

Helena: … I studied History of Art at university. It was really interesting, and the skills I learned are useful. I work in advertising now, and need to have a good understanding of how artistic styles and techniques developed and relate to each other.

Ali: But you don't need to know the history of them, do you?

Helena: I think I do. It's helpful to understand the theory behind the creative side of my work.

Ali: Fair enough. What about you, Felipe? What did you study?

Felipe: Accounting … boring, but practical.

Helena: You're in finance now, aren't you? Do you use your degree in your work?

Felipe: Yes and no. I work for a bank, and did a lot of accounting when I started at the company, but now my job is more connected with marketing. However, having a strong background in accounting really helped to start my career, even if I don't use that knowledge these days.

Helena: What about you Ali? You've got your own software company. Did you study computer science?

Ali: Well, my business designs computer software for small businesses, but I studied Geology.

Helena: Geology? You mean rocks and stones? How did that lead to your career?

Ali: Well, there's more to it than that, but yes. Hmm… I got into computers at university, and then created programmes for an oil company I worked for after I graduated. As I said, in my company we mainly design computer programmes, so nothing to do with my degree, but what I learnt at university has been really useful, too.

Helena: I guess when we were students we couldn't predict which parts of our studies would help us in our career. But they have helped us all, in completely unexpected ways…

🔊 **2.2**

A: So, have you decided what to do when you leave school yet?

B: Well, I might do a university degree, but I don't know what to do. I can't ask my parents to pay for a course that I'm not totally sure about.

A: Have you thought about a MOOC? A massive open online course? They're online courses run by universities, so you can study from home, whenever you want. MOOCs are usually free and anybody can sign up to one. There are often thousands or even hundreds of thousands of students on each course!

B: Wow! Sounds good. How do the universities cover their costs?

A: Err … I'm not sure. Perhaps they sell advertising. If thousands of people visit their website every day, maybe they make money through adverts.

B: Hmm…It must be expensive. If you write an essay, don't they need to pay a professor to assess it?

A: No, students check and grade each other's work. The university tells you how to do it, so you can learn by marking someone else's work.

B: I don't know. I think it's better to get a professor to check your work. Also, you usually have to pass exams to start a regular university course, so you feel the need to finish it. It must be hard to stay motivated with a MOOC.

A: I did read that only about 10% of people who start MOOCs actually finish them. I suppose people sign up for things on the internet all the time if they're free. But 10% of 100,000 students is still a lot. I'm sure it's made a difference in many people's lives.

B: Yeah, I guess you're right. Maybe I will give one a try…

REVIEW TEST 3 ANSWERS

1 1 bacteria 2 viruses 3 microbiomes 4 depression
  5 resistant

2 2 S 3 Q 4 Q 5 S 6 S

3 1 SC 2 DW 3 DW 4 SC 5 DW

4 1 F 2 T 3 F 4 T 5 F

5 1 d 2 g 3 e 4 j 5 a 6 h 7 b 8 f 9 i 10 c

6 2 b; d 3 a; b 4 b; c 5 a; b 6 a; c

REVIEW TEST AUDIOSCRIPTS 3

🔊 **3.1**

Teacher: OK, so today's seminar is about antibiotics. Can anyone tell me what they are?

Student 1: They're a type of medicine that kill bacteria, aren't they? We use them to treat diseases like tuberculosis and typhoid.

Teacher: Yes, that's right.

Student 2: What about the common cold? I heard that antibiotics don't really help with that.

Teacher: Also correct. The common cold is caused by a virus, so antibiotics won't cure it, will they? What are some more general disadvantages of antibiotics?

Student 3: Our bodies need certain bacteria, don't they? I imagine that antibiotics could kill some of those good bacteria too.

Teacher: Absolutely. The technical name for the 'good' bacteria in our bodies is microbiomes. Scientists believe they're essential to our physical and mental health, for example, to help prevent depression.

Student 1: So we should avoid antibiotics altogether then, shouldn't we?

Teacher: Well, no. They can be very effective, but we do need to be careful with them. For example, doctors usually tell you to keep taking antibiotics for a few days, even after you feel better.

Student 2: Yeah … the doctor once said that to me, but I stopped when I was well again. There wasn't any point in continuing, was there?

Teacher: Hmm … the problem is if you stop taking antibiotics before all the bacteria are killed, they'll recover and start reproducing. The next generation of bacteria will be super-strong and a lot more resistant to antibiotics. So the next time you get ill, the antibiotics won't be nearly as effective, will they?

Student 3: So is there anything we can do to …

◄)) 3.2

Host: In today's debate, we'll be discussing homeopathic medicines. First, we'll hear from Siobhan Cooper, who is in favour of homeopathy. Ms Cooper, could you define homeopathic medicines for us, please?

SC: Of course. Homeopathic medicines contain tiny amounts of active substances, which in larger amounts would cause a problem. If a person is suffering from stress, for example, a homeopathic treatment containing typically stress-inducing coffee can actually help them. The body senses the coffee in the medicine, but the amount is so small, and the body's defence reaction so strong, the overall effect is a reduction in stress. It's a powerful principle.

Host: Dr Winston, you are not a supporter of homeopathy. Could you tell us what you think of Ms Cooper's statement?

DW: Thank you. Well, this sounds simple, but again and again experiments show that homeopathic medicines are placebos. A placebo is a false medicine that does nothing. When scientists test a new medicine, they give half the people in the test a placebo – often a sugar tablet – so that they can see if the real medicine actually works. Ms Cooper mentioned that homeopathic medicines contain tiny amounts of active substances, but she didn't say just how tiny. One popular homeopathic medicine, for example, is made from pure water!

Host: Ms Cooper?

SC: First of all, I've heard these arguments many times before. Scientists don't yet understand exactly how homeopathy works, but that doesn't mean it's wrong. Millions of people around the world benefit from homeopathy, but people like Dr Winston only complain about it.

DW: Scientists do understand homeopathy, as I've just explained. Homeopaths make extraordinary claims about their placebo medicines because it's a good way of making money. This is a multi-million dollar industry, which sells sugar and water at ridiculous prices and takes money from people who need real medical help. It is extremely dangerous…

Host: Wow … strong opinions from both sides there…

REVIEW TEST 4 ANSWERS

1 1 plastic helmet 2 strong shoes 3 climbing gloves 4 safety harness 5 metal clips

2 2 Gloves are <u>really</u> important because you have to hold the ropes <u>very</u> tightly.

3 So you are <u>not</u> to take off these gloves at <u>any</u> time – is that <u>clear</u>?

4 … <u>please</u>, when we're putting it on you, you <u>must</u> tell us if it feels uncomfortable!

5 The <u>key</u> thing is that at least <u>one</u> of these clips is to be connected to the safety line at <u>all</u> times.

6 You are <u>not</u> to disconnect <u>both</u> clips at the <u>same</u> time while you're up in the trees.

3 1 tiles 2 slipping (over) 3 outside 4 bags 5 Back 6 20 7 glue 8 fumes 9 window 10 mask

4 1 trek 2 adequate 3 harness 4 slip 5 sunstroke 6 strain 7 apparent 8 collision 9 scald 10 fierce

5 1 You certainly won't make it across the desert without more water.

2 You're unlikely to have any problems if you plan your trip carefully.

3 Be careful on that ladder – you may fall.

4 You're sure to get ill if you inhale those fumes.

5 If you lift that box, you're bound to hurt your back.

REVIEW TEST AUDIOSCRIPTS 4

◄)) 4.1

Hello everybody, welcome to Treetops Rope Park. Before we get started, I need to go through some essential safety instructions. OK, so first, everyone should have a plastic helmet … can you all put it on, please? You need to clip the strap under your chin, and make sure the strap is tight. Has everyone done that? Good.

Right, so the next thing is strong shoes. Some of the bridges are narrow, which can be uncomfortable if the bottoms of your shoes are soft. If anybody needs to change their shoes, please come and speak to me after the talk.

OK, so now put on your climbing gloves, please. Gloves are really important because you have to hold the ropes very tightly and we don't want you to cut your hands. So you are not to take off these gloves at any time. Is that clear?

Right, I still need to explain the most important thing, the safety harness. One of my colleagues will help you put this on, but please, when we're putting it on you, you must tell us if it feels uncomfortable! It shouldn't be too loose or too tight.

Now, these two metal clips here are really important. They attach you to both the safety line and the bridges in each part of the course. The key thing is that at least one of these clips is to be connected to the safety lines at all times. You are not to disconnect both clips at the same time while you're up in the trees. Is that clear? OK, so are there any questions? Right, can you all form a line and follow me…

◄)) 4.2

A: OK Rob, it's all looking pretty good here, but I do need to talk to you about the stairs. What are these broken tiles doing here on the steps?

Rob: Err… I put them there to make more space in the bathroom.

A: Right. Well, first of all, never put anything on the stairs. It creates a real danger of tripping or slipping over. You should try to take waste materials outside immediately.

Rob: Good point, I'll take them outside from now on, although it's easier to take a full bag of tiles out at one time.

A: Hmmm. Well this might be another problem. How heavy is a full bag of broken tiles?

Rob: I don't know … 30 kilograms?

A: As a rule, you should try not to carry any bags that weighs more than about 25 kilograms by yourself, but I'd recommend carrying no more than 20 kilograms of tiles at one time, especially down the stairs. You could really injure your back.

Rob: Really? But I can easily lift 30 or 40 kilos on my own.

A: That's not the point. You really need to look after your back in your job.

Rob: OK, I will. OK, here's the bathroom…

A: It looks great, but it smells like strong glue.

Rob: Yeah, it's tile glue. It smells terrible.

A: Hmmm … that's not good. There's a high risk of inhaling fumes from glue like this in closed spaces. Try to keep the window wide open all the time.

Rob: But when it's raining outside I can't work with the window open!

A: I know, but inhaling fumes is a much more serious problem. You should always wear a mask when working with this glue.

Rob: OK, I've definitely got a mask somewhere. Anything else?

A: Yes. How are you cutting the tiles? …

REVIEW TEST 5 ANSWERS

1 2 d 3 f 4 a 5 b 6 e
2 1 label 2 lacquer 3 reflective layer 4 plastic 5 lacquer
3 1 up/down 2 heat 3 plastic 4 digital 5 applications 6 astronauts 7 digital 8 car 9 parts 10 quickly
4 1 c 2 e 3 a 4 d 5 b
5 1 phase 2 assemble 3 dip 4 seals 5 apply
6 1 e 2 b 3 c 4 b 5 a

REVIEW TEST AUDIOSCRIPTS 5

🔊 **5.1**

OK, so now I'm going to show you the next stage of the CD manufacturing process. You've already seen how we make a master version of the CD, one from which all copies are made. You'll remember that these master versions are covered with very tiny holes and raised areas called 'pits' and 'lands' that store the digital information on the disc. Of course, those pits and lands are far too small for us to see, but they're there and they can be copied.

So the first thing that happens is that the small pieces of plastic, or pellets, you see here go into this heater, to be melted at temperatures of around 300 degrees centigrade. They're then pressed into discs. They already contain all their digital information, but a reflective layer needs to be added so that a CD player can read them. Next, the CDs go into this machine, which we will call the metalizer. As the name suggests, it's where a very thin reflective layer of metal is added on top of the plastic, usually made from aluminium alloys.

After that, we cover the whole disc, top and bottom, in a thin layer of lacquer, which is basically a strong material to protect the disc and the information it contains. When the lacquer has dried, the last thing to add is the label on the top, which is usually painted directly on to the lacquer. It's the most important layer if you want to know whose music you're listening to! It also helps people remember which way up the disc is! OK, so if you'll follow me now, I'll take you to the …

🔊 **5.2**

Our topic today is 3D printing and I'll divide the lecture into two parts. The first part of the talk looks at how 3D printing works. I'll then move on to how it can be used before drawing some conclusions.

OK, let's begin. 3D printing is similar to traditional 2D printing, but of course 2D printers can only print in two dimensions: left–right and forwards–backwards, on a flat surface like paper. 3D printing adds a third dimension, up–down, which means you can print solid objects in whatever shape you want. Some 3D printers work by pointing a powerful laser into a box of powder, which heats it up in particular places to form a solid shape. Other 3D printers shoot out tiny streams of very hot plastic, which then cools to form the desired shape. As you can imagine, the key to successful 3D printing is preparing accurate digital descriptions of the object that you want to print. But once you've got that data ready, you can print as many copies as you want.

Right, so we've looked at how 3D printing works, but what are its practical applications? Let me give you an example. Previously, when astronauts were sent into space, they had to take thousands of spare parts for the machines on the spacecraft, in case anything got broken and needed replacing. Nowadays, all they need is a 3D printer. The astronauts simply download a digital file of the part and print out what they need.

The same principle applies to all sorts of situations. If you're a mechanic and you run a car repair workshop there are also thousands of spare parts that you might need. In the old days, you either needed to keep those in stock or at least know someone who could deliver them quickly. But these days, just like the astronauts, all mechanics need is a 3D printer and some digital files. OK, so now let's talk about conclusions…

REVIEW TEST 6 ANSWERS

1 a 2 b 4 c 1 d 5 e 3
2 1 F 2 T 3 T 4 F 5 F
3 1 c 2 d 3 a 4 e 5 b
4 1 e 2 d 3 b 4 a 5 c
5 1 conservationist 2 orangutan 3 logging; mining 4 copper; diamonds; natural gas 5 coastal regions; rainforest; rescue centre
6 1 adapt 2 exploit 3 survived 4 declined 5 captured
7 2 to 3 from 4 with 5 for 6 than

REVIEW TEST AUDIOSCRIPTS 6

🔊 **6.1**

The subject of my lecture today is the environmental importance of the world's wetlands. First, I'm going to explain why wetlands are important. Then I'll look at some threats to this environment. Finally, I'll talk about some projects to protect the world's wetlands.

Let's begin by defining what we mean by wetlands. Wetlands are characterized by the fact that they support aquatic plant life. Wetlands can be natural or artificial, permanent or temporary, but cannot have water that exceeds a depth of six metres.

So why are they important for us? Wetlands have two key benefits: they remove a lot of carbon from the air, which is vital for reducing the impact of our carbon footprints and climate change, and they are an essential way of storing and regulating water.

Additionally, wetlands contain an enormous range of wildlife. In fact, they are the most diverse of all ecosystems. They are home to about 100,000 species of animals, half of which are insects, and over 20,000 species of fish, mammals, reptiles, amphibians and birds. The plants that live in wetlands hold the soil together, and prevent it from washing away into rivers or the sea. In fact wetland plants are the main protection against flooding in many countries around the world. When wetlands are drained, the results can be disastrous. One reason Hurricane Katrina caused so much damage to the city of New Orleans in 2005 was that the wetlands around the Mississippi River had been drained.

This is one of many ways in which human activity is destroying wetlands. In fact, it has been claimed that environmental damage is more prominent within wetland systems than any other ecosystem on Earth. A second way in which we are destroying wetlands is through …

◀)) 6.2

The Great Pacific Garbage Patch, or GPGP, is an area of the Pacific Ocean with an extremely high concentration of plastic, chemical waste and rubbish. It covers an area of 15 million square kilometres, and is more than twice the size of the USA. However, it's difficult to be exact about this because most of the plastic particles are too small to be seen by the naked eye.

The oceans of the world flow in a series of circles thousands of kilometres wide. The GPGP has formed at the centre of one of the largest circles, so rubbish from all over the Pacific Ocean is pulled into its centre. There's a huge amount of waste in the GPGP from ships – a typical passenger cruise ship generates around 3,000 tonnes of waste every week.

The GPGP was discovered in 1997 by a sailor, Charles Moore. As he sailed through it, he found plastic rubbish floating as far as the eye could see. It took him a whole week to sail from one side of the patch to the other.

It's clear that large pieces of plastic, like bags, cause serious environmental problems, for example when eaten by birds. But the real danger with the GPGP comes from invisible particles of plastic, which are eaten by tiny sea creatures. These animals are then eaten by fish, causing highly poisonous chemicals to spread through all ocean wildlife.

So how can we clean up the GPGP? One promising idea is to use a series of connected platforms to collect the waste. The ocean's own currents should push the waste towards these platforms, where it can be collected and recycled. If this idea works, the whole area could be cleaned within five years, and possibly even at a profit. Let's look now more closely at this idea …

REVIEW TEST 7 ANSWERS

1 1F 2T 3T 4T 5F 6F 7T 8T 9F 10F
2 2 owner S architect T
3 owner S architect S
4 owner S architect S
5 owner T architect S
6 owner T architect T
3 1 g 2 j 3 e 4 b 5 i 6 c 7 d 8 a 9 f 10 h
4 2 arranged 3 promised 4 expect 5 envisage
6 anticipate

REVIEW TEST AUDIOSCRIPTS 7

◀)) 7.1

The city of Putrajaya in Malaysia is home to some of the most exciting architecture in the world. It's a city designed by architects and planners, rather than one that has developed naturally over hundreds of years. The city was created in 1995 to reduce the overcrowding in Kuala Lumpur, 25km to the north. Since then, it has become the centre of government and administration for Malaysia, but the country's capital is still Kuala Lumpur.

The city is built on two design principles: it is both a garden city and an intelligent city. As a garden city, nature, the environment and green space are fundamental to the design of all the city's layout and all of its buildings. 40% of the city's land is parks, lakes, botanical gardens and large areas of wetland. Many of the city's buildings have also been designed to have a low impact on the local and global environment.

As an intelligent city, the latest information and communication technologies have been built right into the buildings. More importantly, the architecture of the city aims to encourage the networking and sharing of ideas between the people who live there. The city is designed to bring people together, not keep them apart as in so many cities.

The buildings of Putrajaya incorporate the best of modern architecture, but include elements of the traditional architecture of this part of the world. In the heart of the city is the Dataran Putra, a huge open space with a star design in its centre. The city skyline is dominated by the beautiful Seri Wawasan Bridge, whose central tower is shaped like a ship. Another impressive building is the Istana Melawati, a royal palace with three tall towers, based on the design of towers in traditional Malay palaces. The roofs of the towers use traditional designs…

◀)) 7.2

Owner: So, welcome to the Riverside Hotel. What do you think?

Architect: Well, it's a nice old building in a good location. But it's in a pretty bad condition.

Owner: Yes, that's why I bought it. It was cheap, and I'm convinced there's potential to turn it into a really beautiful hotel.

Architect: Yes, I suppose it depends how long before you want to open. I mean, if you want to open three months from now, we could probably clean it up by then, but I can't really say for sure without inspecting the building carefully.

Owner: Don't worry, I'm sure 3 months is more than enough time.

Architect: OK, but if you want to do something really amazing here, and I think you should, then I strongly recommend that you plan to do it over at least a year.

Owner: Hmm. That's a long time. When you say 'amazing', what did you have in mind?

Architect: Well, for example, this entrance lobby is quite small and dark. Have you considered putting in a glass roof? I really feel that would make a lot of difference here.

Owner: I agree completely. I had the same idea.

Architect: You should also knock down these walls to make the entrance much bigger. If you want the entrance to be amazing, it's got to be big.

Owner: Err … maybe you're right. What else did you have in mind for the entrance?

Architect: How about a wide staircase over there … perhaps made of glass?

Owner: Err … I'm not sure about that. I was thinking of having a lift, not stairs.

Architect: Ah, but the stairs would actually be more…

REVIEW TEST 8 ANSWERS

1 1 5000 2 fitness 3 turbine 4 mouse 5 drinking water
2 1 nervousness 2 excitement 3 surprise 4 annoyance 5 sadness
3 1 40 2 30 3 15 4 30 5 8 6 11 7 24 8 1 9 5 10 20
4

	1↓
2→	C H A L L E N G E
3→	P O T E N T I A L
4→	F U N C T I O N
5→	M A I N T E N A N C E
6→	R E S E R V O I R
7→	D R A W B A C K
8→	C O N S U M P T I O N
9→	C A P A C I T Y
10→	V O L U M E
11→	M A I N L A N D

5 1 b 2 a 3 d 4 b 5 c

REVIEW TEST AUDIOSCRIPTS 8

◀)) **8.1**

A: Hello everybody. Thanks for coming. As you know, the purpose of today's meeting is to discuss how we can generate our own electricity here at the college. I've asked each of you to research the different options we have. Laura, maybe you could start by telling us about 'people power'?

Laura: Sure. Well, the idea here is that we've got 5,000 students here at the college, so we could use the energy of these students to create electricity by making it fun. I've checked on the internet, and you can buy fitness equipment, like running machines and exercise bikes, which actually generate electricity. If students want to get fit anyway, why not generate power at the same time?

C: But how would that work? I mean, I can imagine how an exercise bike could generate electricity, with a turbine connected to it. But a running machine?

Laura: Well, you know you can get a wheel for a pet mouse to run inside? As the mouse runs, the wheel turns. Now you can buy a similar, giant wheel for people, which drives a turbine to generate power.

A: Hmm … I read about something similar. Some children's roundabouts in Africa pumped drinking water out of the ground while children were playing on them. The problem was, people wanted a normal pump to give them water, not a children's toy.

Laura: Well, this is different. Those people really needed water, the problem was that the roundabout was the only way of getting it. We're in a better position – we've got electricity from other sources if we need it, but there's no reason why we couldn't generate more while we're getting fit.

A: OK, good point. So how much electricity would this fitness equipment generate? And how much does it cost…

◀)) **8.2** **8**

Hello, and welcome to the programme. Today we're in Dubai to find out about the city's plans to become more energy-efficient. Not so long ago, Dubai's extraordinary economic growth meant that people could use as much electricity as they wanted without worrying about its cost or environmental impact. For example, with temperatures that regularly go over 40 degrees during the day, and often stay above 30 degrees at night, many people keep air conditioning systems on all day and all night. Add to this skiing complexes with artificial snow, amazing real estate projects like the construction of the world's tallest building, and a successful tourist industry, and you can imagine how much electricity the city gets through.

But, this is changing, and Dubai looks set to become a lot more energy-efficient over the next 15 years. The city plans to cut its energy and water usage by 30%, mainly by making buildings, and there are also plans for government cars, to run on compressed gas, which is much less harmful to the environment than petrol.

But the real potential for energy-efficiency in a place like Dubai comes from the fact that it enjoys between eight and 11 hours of sunshine all year round. This sunshine could be turned into electricity. The newly-opened Solar Park at Seih Al Dahal can generate 24 million kilowatt hours of electricity per year and will soon provide 1% of the city's energy needs. This will rise to 5% by 2030, by which point the Solar Park is expected to cover over 20 square kilometres of desert.

Even this is only the beginning. In fact, some experts have claimed that solar energy in Dubai has the potential to provide more than twice Dubai's current electricity consumption …

REVIEW TEST 9 ANSWERS

1 1 C 2 H 3 A 4 H 5 A 6 C 7 C 8 V 9 V 10 V
2 Points mentioned: 1, 2, 5, 8, 10
3 2 rejected 3 removed 4 appreciate 5 interpret 6 junction 7 self-expression 8 inspiration 9 restores 10 commented 11 focus
4 1 reality 2 granted 3 matter 4 as 5 actually

REVIEW TEST AUDIOSCRIPTS 9

◀)) **9.1**

Host: Hello and welcome to today's show. Today, we're at the National Museum, where an exhibition of paintings by Scottish artist Tyrone Long starts today. I'm joined now by art critic Walter McGregor. Mr. McGregor, tell us about the paintings in this exhibition.

Art critic: Good morning. Well, these paintings were done at a time in Long's life when he was depressed and sad, and I think those emotions are clear in his work.

Host: Really? They almost look like something a small child might paint to me. I mean, what are they of?

Art critic: We don't know. The artist never liked to explain his work. He didn't want to tell people what his paintings showed.

Host: Right. I think I prefer to know what I'm looking at. Can you explain why all the paintings are green?

Art critic: We know that Long was unhappy in New York, where he was living at the time, so perhaps the paintings say that he missed the green hills and fields of home. That's what makes his work so interesting – we all take our own stories from the paintings.

Host: Right, I see. OK, thank you Mr. McGregor. Now I'd like to talk to a visitor to the exhibition. Can I ask what you think of the paintings?

Visitor: I love the colours. They make me feel good and they're very relaxing.

Host: And what do you see when you look at the pictures?

Visitor: Well, this area looks like it could be the sea, and these lines remind me of a horse.

Host: A green horse? In the sea? Really?

Visitor: I'm not sure you need to think too much about what the picture shows. It's more about how it makes you feel.

Host: OK, thanks a lot for that. Now let's speak to another visitor…

◀)) 9.2

A: OK, now, the next item on the agenda is the furniture in the reception area and waiting rooms. As you know, we want to create the impression that our medical centre is stylish and technologically advanced. Our current furniture feels a bit old-fashioned, so I'm proposing that we replace some of it with these chairs. As you can see from the image, they're made of metal and clear plastic, which looks really modern. And I love their geometric shape.

B: Can I just say something? To my mind, the most important feature isn't what the chairs look like, but how comfortable they are. This is a medical centre, not an art gallery. People just want somewhere comfortable to sit.

A: I'm afraid I disagree with you there. Our patients have to believe that our doctors and all of our equipment is of the highest quality. That means managing their impression of us from the moment they walk through the door. If the reception area looks old-fashioned, they may not have confidence in our medical skills. That's not just my opinion, 42% of our patients complained that the reception area creates the wrong impression – that's much too high.

B: I agree that we need to make it look better. The current furniture is ten years old and we definitely need to replace it. But all I'm saying is that comfort needs to come first. Those chairs look like they've come from a spaceship – very modern but really uncomfortable. I wouldn't want to sit on them, especially if I was ill.

A: Really? I think they actually look quite …

REVIEW TEST 10 ANSWERS

1 1 50 2 motorbike 3 changes 4 time 5 children 6 fun
7 60 8 electric guitar 9 world 10 novel

2

	1950s	1986	1994	1998	2003	2011
Men	60	65	57	61	58	64
Women	67	74	71	73	72	75

3 1 c 2 e 3 d 4 a 5 b

4 1 devote 2 contribute 3 participate 4 assist 5 indicate

5 1 b 2 a 3 c 4 b 5 d

REVIEW TEST AUDIOSCRIPTS 10

◀)) 10.1

Sonia: Hey look, is that Professor Philips? It looks like him but he's riding a motorbike, so maybe it isn't. I mean, he must be about 50 years old.

Mike: It's definitely him. That motorbike's his new toy. I think he's going through a midlife crisis.

Sonia: A midlife crisis? What's that?

Mike: Err … it's when someone suddenly realizes they're getting older and decides to make big life changes. People of that age have often spent years having to work and look after their children, and then suddenly when they're in their fifties, they've got spare time and money, and their children have left home. So they can have fun for the first time in a long time.

Sonia: So they go out and buy a motorbike?

Mike: Sometimes, but not always. My uncle, who's nearly 60, just bought an expensive electric guitar – I guess he decided he wants to be a rock star or something.

Sonia: Wow. Sounds like a good idea to me. But why is it called a midlife *crisis*? It sounds nice, not a crisis at all.

Mike: Well, I guess that's because some people suddenly worry they've spent too much of their lives doing ordinary things and not doing something more meaningful. I mean, everyone wants to do something more than just going to work and watching TV in their life. So they make big changes, like deciding to travel around the world… or buying a motorbike!

Sonia: Sounds like my mother – she's writing a novel at the moment. She says it's something she's always wanted to do, but never had the time to before.

Mike: Good for her. I think that's a really nice idea.

Sonia: Yeah, me too. So what do you think you'll do when …

◀)) 10.2

OK, so I'd like to talk about changes in life expectancy in my country, Russia. In the 1950s, life expectancy for men was 60, rising to a peak of 65 in 1986. However, in the early 1990s, men started dying much younger. By 1994, life expectancy for men was down to 57. This was clearly the result of the dramatic political and economic changes in Russia around the time.

Things had improved slightly by 1998, when male life expectancy was up to 61, but then it fell back to 58 in 2003 – these were still difficult times for my country. Fortunately, male life expectancy has risen steadily since 2003, up to 64 in 2011, nearly at the same age as 1986. This is still quite low compared to other countries, but at least the trend is more positive than it was.

Women in Russia tend to live around ten years longer than men, a difference that is much bigger than in most other countries. One possible reason for this is that men in Russia often do dangerous physical work in hard conditions and have many accidents. The life expectancy graph shows a similar shape for both men and women, although it is rather less dramatic. In the 1950s, women could expect to live to 67, rising to 74 in 1986. This decreased to 71 in 1993, at the same time as life expectancy for men showed that dramatic fall. Women's life expectancy went back up to 73 in 1998, but then fell back to 72 in 2004. It then rose steadily over the next few years, reaching a peak of 75 in 2011. Let's hope this trend continues, and that the life expectancy of both men and women keeps rising…

Name: .... **Date:** ....

LISTENING (20 marks)

LISTENING 1

1 (🔊 **1.1**) Listen to the presentation and complete the pie charts with a percentage (e.g. 20%). 1 mark for each correct answer.

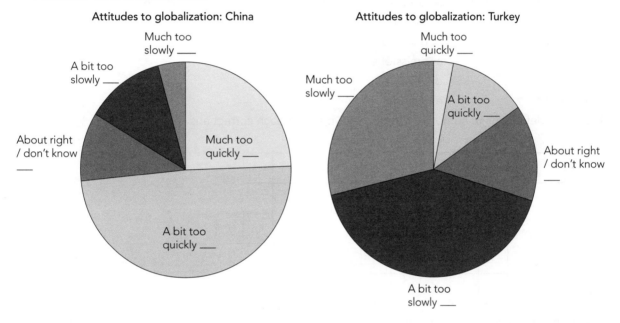

Attitudes to globalization: China

Attitudes to globalization: Turkey

LISTENING 2

2 (🔊 **1.2**) Listen to a radio programme about globalization and culture. Choose the correct option (a–c) to complete the statements. 2 marks for each correct answer.

1 The cultural changes as a result of globalization …

  a … are mostly bad.

  b … are a mixture of good and bad.

  c … are mostly good.

2 A possible problem with American culture is that …

  a … it means people don't have enough contact with their own culture.

  b … it is old-fashioned and boring.

  c … young people might stop being interested in their own culture.

3 These days, most people around the world …

  a … are only interested in American culture.

  b … still spend at least half their time interacting with their own culture.

  c … are no longer interested in American culture.

4 Dr Martin is excited because …

    a … American culture is becoming less popular.

    b … she expects to see films and music coming from many countries in future.

    c … the internet has made it easier to listen to music and watch films.

5 Dr Martin says that true globalization …

    a … will never happen.

    b … only involves American culture.

    c … is going to start soon.

LANGUAGE DEVELOPMENT (15 marks)

3 Match the words to make phrases from this unit. 1 mark for each correct answer.

1	carbon dioxide	a	footprint
2	carbon	b	paddies
3	climate	c	emissions
4	rice	d	chain
5	supply	e	change

4 Use the definitions to complete the puzzle. 1 mark for each correct answer.

1↓

2→ [ ][ ][ ][ ][C][ ][ ][ ][ ][ ]
3→ [ ][R][ ][ ][ ][ ]
4→ [ ][O][ ][ ][ ][ ][ ][ ]
5→ [ ][P][ ][ ][ ][ ]
6→ [ ][ ][ ][S][ ][ ][ ][ ]

1 Plants that are grown on a farm

2 Another name for farming

3 To buy something, especially for business

4 Turning a natural food into a manufactured product

5 Brought from another country

6 People who buy and use a product

5 Complete the second sentence in each pair so that it means the same as the first. Use the passive voice. Don't use the words in (brackets). 1 mark for each correct answer.

1 (They) often transport food by aeroplane.

   Food _____ by aeroplane.

2 (People) should pay farmers in poor countries more for the food that they produce.

   Farmers in poor countries _____ for the food that they produce.

3 (Shops) all over the world sell agricultural products from my country.

   Agricultural products from my country _____ all over the world.

4 (You) can reduce your carbon footprint if you eat local foods.

   Your carbon footprint _____ if you eat local foods.

5 (We) didn't import these vegetables – they're from this country.

   These vegetables _____ – they're from this country.

TOTAL ___ / 35

REVIEW TEST 2

Name: .... **Date:** ....

LISTENING (20 marks)

LISTENING 1

1 🔊 **2.1** Listen to three people discussing how their university courses have affected their careers and complete the table. 1 mark for each correct answer.

	Studied	Current job
Helena	_History_ of _Art_	Works in ¹ _____
Felipe	² _____	Works for a ³ _____
Ali	⁴ _____	Owns a ⁵ _____ company

2 🔊 **2.1** Listen again. Write Helena (H), Felipe (F) or Ali (A) next to the staements. 1 mark for each correct answer.

1 I don't use my knowledge from university any more. _____

2 The subject I studied isn't as simple as you might expect. _____

3 I got into my current career when I was studying. _____

4 It's useful to know the theory behind my daily work. _____

5 My studies helped me to get my first job. _____

LISTENING 2

3 🔊 **2.2** Listen to a conversation about MOOCs (massive open online courses). Write certain (C) or uncertain (U) next to the statements. 1 mark for each correct answer.

1 You can study whenever you want. _____

2 MOOCs cover their costs by selling advertising. _____

3 It's good for students to check each other's work. _____

4 Many students lack motivation for studying MOOCs. _____

5 A large number of people fail to complete MOOCs. _____

4 🔊 **2.2** Listen again and choose the correct answer, a or b. 1 mark for each correct answer.

1 Who are the two people talking?

  a A university student talking to his mum.

  b A school student talking to his older cousin.

2 Why is the male speaker not sure about going to university?

  a Because he feels uncomfortable with the idea of asking his parents to pay for it.

  b Because he would find it hard to stay motivated in a traditional course.

3 What is the female speaker's purpose?

  a To persuade the male speaker to join a MOOC.

  b To warn the male speaker about the problems with online learning.

4 What is the male speaker's opinion about essay marking?

  a A computer can mark writing more accurately than a professor.

  b A professor should mark an essay rather than a computer.

5 What is the female speaker's opinion on the number of people who don't finish MOOCs?

  a It isn't necessarily a problem.

  b It suggests that many MOOCs are too difficult.

LANGUAGE DEVELOPMENT (15 marks)

5 Complete the sentences using words from the box. 1 mark for each correct answer.

> exhausted   acquire   complex   in-depth   specialist   career
> theoretical   vocational   weightless   apprentice

1 Her course is too _____– she isn't learning any practical skills.

2 We're conducting an _____ analysis of the causes of these social changes.

3 I had three exams on the same day – by the end, I was completely _____.

4 He's an excellent lecturer – when he talks about _____ subjects, he makes them sound really simple.

5 People can fly around inside spacecraft because they are _____.

6 I'm going on a training course because I want to _____ some new skills.

7 He's looking for a course that will help him in his long-term _____, not just a job to earn money.

8 In my country, before you can be an electrician, you need to spend at least one year as an _____.

9 After completing a four-year degree in medicine, most people spend another three years training to be a _____ in a particular field of medicine.

10 She wants to go to a _____ college to learn some very practical skills.

6 Read the sentences. Correct the mistakes in the wrong sentences. 1 mark for each correct answer.

1 Where you would prefer to study?

2 I'd like to know more about the course.

3 I'd rather if you asked your teacher, not me.

4 Would you prefer a practical course or a theoretical one?

5 Would you rather to do a 3- or 4-year course?

TOTAL ___ / 35

Name: .... **Date:** ....

LISTENING (20 marks)

LISTENING 1

1 (◄) 3.1 Listen to a seminar about antibiotics and complete the notes with words from the box. There are some words that you don't need. 1 mark for each correct answer.

anxiety   bacteria   dangerous   depression   microbiomes   nerves   resistant   viruses

Antibiotics

Treat diseases caused by [1] _____ (e.g. tuberculosis, typhoid)

Don't help with illnesses caused by [2] _____ (e.g. common cold)

Disadvantages of antibiotics:

1 They may cause damage to [3] _____ – important for physical and mental health. (e.g. prevent [4] _____)

2 If you stop taking antibiotics too early, the remaining bacteria become more [5] _____ to them.

2 Listen to the sentences. Write question (Q) or statement (S) next to the sentences below. The first one has been done for you. 1 mark for each correct answer.

1 They're a type of medicine that kill bacteria, aren't they? _____Q_____

2 Antibiotics won't cure it, will they? _____

3 Our bodies need certain bacteria, don't they? _____

4 So we should avoid antibiotics altogether then, shouldn't we? _____

5 There wasn't any point in continuing, was there? _____

6 The antibiotics won't be nearly as effective, will they? _____

LISTENING 2

3 (◄) 3.2 Listen to the beginning of a debate about homeopathy, a form of alternative medicine. Write Siobhan Cooper (SC) or Dr Winston (DW) for each opinion. 1 mark for each correct answer.

Siobhan Cooper is a registered homeopath. She gives presentations about homeopathy and runs homeopathic training courses. Dr Charles Winston is a member of a regional doctors' association. He also works as a consultant for large pharmaceutical companies.

1 Homeopathy gets the body to fight an active substance. _____

2 A placebo works because people believe it is a real medicine. _____

3 Some placebo medicines are made of sugar. _____

4 Millions of people around the world benefit from homeopathy. _____

5 Some companies are make a lot of money out of homeopathy. _____

4 Write true (*T*) or false (*F*) next to the statements. 1 mark for each correct answer.

1 Ms Cooper says that large amounts of coffee help with stress. _____

2 Dr Winston says that scientists use placebos to test if medicines work. _____

3 Ms Cooper is surprised by Dr Winston's arguments. _____

4 Ms Cooper says that scientists don't understand homeopathy. _____

5 Dr Winston believes homeopathic medicines are good value for money. _____

LANGUAGE DEVELOPMENT (15 marks)

5 Match the sentence halves. Use the words in bold to help you. 1 mark for each correct answer.

1 The doctor gave me some

2 The link between smoking and cancer has been

3 They analysed the bacteria under **controlled**

4 I felt much better but they kept me in hospital for the night

5 People can **contract**

6 Pharmaceutical companies conduct **clinical**

7 She was very ill but made a full

8 **Researchers** are trying to understand how the **outbreak**

9 We need to collect more

10 He caught anthrax when he **inhaled**

a **diseases** when they travel to other countries.

b **recovery** after a few weeks.

c some **spores**.

d **antibiotics** to treat my infection.

e conditions in a laboratory.

f **occurred**.

g **proven** in many studies.

h **trials** before launching a new medicine.

i **data** before we can be sure of the causes of the disease.

j as a **precaution**.

6 Choose the two correct expressions (a–d) to complete the sentences. 1 mark for each correct answer.

1 She noticed a pain in her side _____ she was walking.

a until   (b after)   (c while)   d up to

2 She had problems with her heart _____ the age of six, and then she recovered.

a after   b up to   c as of   d until

3 He became ill _____ a trip to Thailand.

a during   b after   c up to   d until

4 I haven't had any problems _____ my operation.

a while   b since   c after   d before

5 _____ tomorrow, I'm going to go running every day.

a as of   b from   c throughout   d before

6 Don't worry. You'll be asleep _____ the operation.

a during   b as of   c throughout   d since

TOTAL ___ / 35

Name: .... **Date:** ....

LISTENING (20 marks)

LISTENING 1

1 (🔊 4.1) Listen to a safety presentation in a rope park. Use the words in the box to make safety equipment collocations. 1 mark for each correct answer.

> climbing clips gloves harness helmet
> metal plastic safety shoes strong

1 _____ _____

2 _____ _____

3 _____ _____

4 _____ _____

5 _____ _____

2 (🔊 4.1) Listen again. Underline the stressed words in each sentence. The number in brackets tells you how many words to underline. The first one has been done for you. 1 mark for each correct answer.

1 You need to clip the strap under your chin, and make <u>sure</u> the <u>strap</u> is tight. (2)

2 Gloves are really important because you have to hold the ropes very tightly. (2)

3 So you are not to take off these gloves at any time – is that clear? (3)

4 … please, when we're putting it on you, you must tell us if it feels uncomfortable! (2)

5 The key thing is that at least one of these clips is to be connected to the safety line at all times. (3)

6 You are not to disconnect both clips at the same time while you're up in the trees. (3)

LISTENING 2

3 (🔊 4.2) Listen to a house-building risk assessment meeting and complete the table. 1 mark for each correct answer.

Hazard	Risk	Risk reduction
Broken [1] _____ on the stairs	Tripping or [2] _____ over	Always take waste materials [3] _____ immediately
Carrying heavy [4] _____	[5] _____ injury	Carry no more than [6] _____ kg of tiles
Smell of [7] _____	[8] Inhaling _____	Keep [9] _____ wide open and wear a [10] _____

LANGUAGE DEVELOPMENT (15 marks)

4 Complete the definitions with words from the box. There are some words that you don't need. 1 mark for each correct answer.

> adequate sunstroke trek sunburn goggles collision harness
> straightforward helmet apparent potential scald fierce slip strain

1 If you _____, you go for a long hard walk.

2 If your preparation for a trip is _____, you have done enough.

3 A _____ is a piece of safety equipment to hold your body in place.

4 If you _____, you fall because you stand on something wet.

5 _____ is a medical condition caused by being very hot.

6 You might _____ your back if you lift something that is too heavy.

7 If a risk is very _____, you can see it clearly.

8 You might have a _____ with another vehicle if you don't keep your eyes on the road.

9 If you _____ yourself, you are hurt by very hot water or steam.

10 A _____ storm is very strong and violent.

5 Complete the second sentence in each pair so that it means the same as the first. Use the word in brackets. 1 mark for each correct answer.

1 You're certain not to make it across the desert without more water. (won't)

You certainly _____across the desert without more water.

2 I don't think you'll have any problems if you plan your trip carefully. (unlikely)

You're _____ any problems if you plan your trip carefully.

3 Be careful on that ladder – there's a risk of falling. (may)

Be careful on that ladder – you _____.

4 I'm sure you'll get ill if you inhale those fumes. (sure to)

_____ to get ill if you inhale those fumes.

5 You'll definitely hurt your back if you try to lift that box. (bound)

If you lift that box, _____ your back.

TOTAL ___ / 35

REVIEW TEST 5

Name: .... Date: ....

LISTENING (20 marks)

LISTENING 1

1 (🔊 **5.1**) Listen to part of a tour of a CD factory. Match the sentence halves. The first one is done for you. 1 mark for each correct answer.

1 The CDs are all copies of ———————————————————
2 The digital information on the CDs is stored in tiny
3 The plastic discs are made from pellets
4 The CDs go through a machine called
5 A thin, reflective layer of metal is added, usually made of
6 The CDs are covered with a strong material called

a a metalizer.
b aluminium alloys.
c a master version.
d holes called pits and lands.
e lacquer.
f melted at 300°C.

2 (🔊 **5.1**) Listen again. Complete the diagram of a CD with words from the box. Layer 1 is the top of the CD. You need to use one word twice. 1 mark for each correct answer.

| plastic disc   lacquer   reflective layer   label |

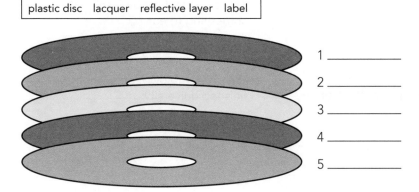

1 _____
2 _____
3 _____
4 _____
5 _____

LISTENING 2

3 (🔊 **5.2**) Listen to a lecture about 3D-printing and complete the notes. 1 mark for each correct answer.

A: How 3D-printing works

- 2D printers work in two dimensions: left–right and forwards–backwards
- 3D printers add 3rd dimension to the process: [1] _____–_____
- Type 1: point a laser into box of powder to [2] _____ it up
- Type 2: shoot out streams of hot [3] _____, which then cools
- Key to successful printing: accurate [4] _____ descriptions

B: Practical [5] _____: what can 3D-printing be used for?

- Example 1: [6] _____ now take a 3D printer and [7] _____ files into space.
- Example 2: [8] _____ repair workshops used to need thousands of spare [9] _____ – either kept in stock or delivered [10] _____. Now, with 3D printers, not needed.

LANGUAGE DEVELOPMENT (15 marks)

4 Match the words to make expressions from unit. 1 mark for each correct answer.

1	mass-	a	quality
2	small-	b	together
3	high-	c	produced
4	hand	d	made
5	put	e	scale

5 Complete the text with the words from the box. 1 mark for each correct answer.

apply   assemble   dip   phase   seals

> We make these decorations by hand, so our production volume is very small – only about 20 items per day. In the first ^{1}_____ of the production process, we ^{2}_____ the decorations out of five parts of wood. Next, we ^{3}_____ them in this paint, which makes them look good and also ^{4}_____ the wood inside, to protect it from water. Finally, we ^{5}_____ a final coat of sealant, which protects the decoration from being scratched.

6 Match the sentences on the left (1– 5) with the explanations (a– e) on the right. 1 mark for each correct answer.

1 To get a job in this factory, you need to have good qualifications.

2 You must keep this door locked.

3 You have to keep this door locked.

4 You don't have to bring food or drink into the factory.

5 You mustn't bring food or drink into the factory.

a It's against the rules.

b There's a machine here so you can buy something to eat.

c I don't know why but it's the rule.

d I'll be very angry if I find it open.

e We only employ people who have finished university.

TOTAL ___ / 35

Name: .... Date: ....

LISTENING (20 marks)

LISTENING 1

1 (🔊 6.1) Listen to a lecture about the importance of wetlands. Number the topics in the order you hear them. 1 mark for each correct answer.

a The importance of wetlands for humans _____

b The connection between wetlands and hurricane damage _____

c A definition of wetlands _____

d The level of damage to wetland ecosystems _____

e The range of animals and plants living in wetlands _____

2 (🔊 6.1) Listen to the lecture again. Write true (T) or false (F) next to the statements. 1 mark for each correct answer.

1 An area of land which is covered in 10 metres of water is classed as wetland. _____

2 Wetlands play an important role in reducing climate change. _____

3 There are around 50,000 insect species living in wetlands around the world. _____

4 The Mississippi River wetlands were in good condition before Hurricane Katrina. _____

5 Humans have had very little impact on most wetland ecosystems. _____

LISTENING 2

3 (🔊 6.2) Listen to a talk about the Great Pacific Garbage Patch (GPGP). Match the parts of the presentation (1–5) with the ideas (a–e) from the talk. 1 mark for each correct answer.

Giving background information	1
	2
	3
Explaining a problem	4
Offering a solution	5

a The discovery of the GPGP

b Cleaning up the GPGP

c The size of the GPGP

d The formation of the GPGP

e The effect of plastic on animals

4 (🔊 7.2) Match the details with the ideas (a–e) in Exercise 3. 1 mark for each correct answer.

a The smallest particles are even more dangerous than the large ones. _____

b Ships generate a lot of waste. _____

c Removing the plastic may not be too expensive. _____

d A sailor spent several days sailing through the GPGP. _____

e A lot of the plastic isn't big enough to see. _____

LANGUAGE DEVELOPMENT (15 marks)

5 Look at the descriptions and write the word or words from the box. There are some words that you don't need. 1 mark for each correct answer.

> source   coastal regions   rescue centre
> mining   conservationist   copper   dust
> storm   diamonds   logging   natural gas
> orangutan   rainforest   destruction

1 A person: _____

2 An example of an endangered species: _____

3 Two activities which lead to the destruction of natural habitats: _____ / _____

4 Three examples of minerals or natural resources: _____ / _____ / _____

5 Three places where animals live: _____ / _____ / _____

6 Complete the sentences with the correct form of the verbs from the box. 1 mark for each correct answer.

> capture   adapt   decline   exploit   survive

1 As sea temperatures rise, it can be difficult for fish species to _____ to the new conditions.

2 When people _____ natural resources, they can do a lot of damage to the environment.

3 Many animals died in the fire. Only about 20% of them _____.

4 The number of species of plant in this part of the world has _____ greatly in recent years – there are now only half as many as 20 years ago.

5 This lion was _____ in Africa when he was a baby.

7 Complete the text with a word in each space. 1 mark for each correct answer.

> According ¹ _to_ a recent report, the populations of around 75% of animal species in this country are declining due ²_____ human activities. Apart ³_____ obvious causes such as hunting, the main reasons for the decline appear to be habitat destruction, together ⁴_____ pollution. This problem affects all parts of the country, except ⁵_____ the mountains in the far north, where, rather ⁶_____ declining, animal populations are actually growing.

TOTAL ___ / 35

Name: .... Date: ....

LISTENING (20 marks)

LISTENING 1

1 (◀ 7.1) Listen to a radio programme about the architecture of Putrakjaya, a city in Malaysia. Write true (T) or false (F) next to the statements. 1 mark for each correct answer.

1 Putrajaya developed over a period of hundreds of years. _____

2 The city is 25km south of the capital. _____

3 Putrajaya is the administrative centre of Malaysia. _____

4 Putrajaya is a 'garden city' because green space is part of its design. _____

5 Over half of the city consists of green space. _____

6 Putrajaya is decribed as an intelligent city because its people are so creative. _____

7 It is easy to meet other people in the city and share ideas. _____

8 The architecture of Putrajaya is a mixture of old and new ideas. _____

9 Dataran Putra has a tall tower in the centre. _____

10 The Seri Wawasan Bridge tower is shaped like a palace. _____

LISTENING 2

2 (◀ 7.2) Listen to a discussion between the owner of a hotel and an architect developing the hotel. Write strong (S) or tentative (T) next to the opinions and suggestions. The first one is done for you. 2 marks for each correct answer.

	owner	architect
1 There's potential to turn it into a really beautiful hotel.	S	T
2 They could clean the hotel up in three months.		
3 They should spend at least a year making the hotel 'amazing'.		
4 They should put in a new glass roof above the lobby.		
5 They should make the lobby area much bigger.		
6 There should be a glass staircase in the lobby area.		

LANGUAGE DEVELOPMENT (15 marks)

3 Match the sentence halves. 1 mark for each correct answer.

1 If you are concerned about something,	a some people may not like it.
2 If a building has weak foundations,	b it will be difficult to achieve.
3 If you recognise a landmark,	c you don't replace them.
4 If a plan is very ambitious,	d you change it completely.
5 If a design is very contemporary,	e you can often work out where you are.
6 If you preserve some features of a building,	f you will need to clear away remains of the old buildings first.
7 If you transform a building,	g you are worried about it.
8 If a design is controversial,	h it becomes yours, usually because you have bought it.
9 If you want to build on wasteland,	
10 If you acquire a property,	i it is modern and up-to-date.
	j it might collapse.

4 Rearrange the letters in brackets to make a verb with a future meaning. Complete the sentences. 1 mark for each correct answer.

1 Our client ___intends___ to rebuild this warehouse. (tiensdn)

2 They have _____ to meet us tomorrow afternoon. (geardran)

3 The developer has _____ to ensure that the new building fits in with the existing architecture. (emprsdoi)

4 We _____ to complete the building within two months. (cxepet)

5 We don't _____ removing any of the building's original features. (vgneiesa)

6 The builders didn't _____ the walls being so thick. (eaitpancti)

TOTAL ___ / 35

REVIEW TEST 8

Name: .... Date: ....

LISTENING (20 marks)

LISTENING 1

1 (◀)) **8.1** Listen to a meeting about energy generation. Complete the sentences with a word or number. 1 mark for each correct answer.

1 There are _____ students at the college.

2 Electricity can be generated using _____ equipment such as running machines and exercise bikes.

3 An exercise bike can generate electricity with a _____ connected to it.

4 The running machine is like a large version of a wheel for a _____.

5 Play roundabouts in Africa were used to provide _____.

2 (◀)) **8.1** Listen again. Write the emotion from the box next to the sentence. 1 mark for each correct answer.

| annoyance   sadness   excitement   nervousness   surprise |

1 The purpose of today's meeting is to plan how we can generate our own electricity … _____

2 We could use the energy of these students to create electricity by making it fun. _____

3 But a running machine? _____

4 … people wanted a normal pump to give them water, not a children's toy. _____

5 Those people really needed water … _____

LISTENING 2

3 (◀)) **8.2** Listen to a radio programme about energy use in Dubai and complete the fact file. 1 mark for each correct answer.

> **Dubai: energy use and energy solutions**
>
> Temperatures in Dubai: over ^{1} _____ °C during the day, and up to ^{2} _____ °C at night.
>
> Energy efficiency plan for Dubai: over next ^{3} _____ years, cut energy and water usage by ^{4} _____%.
>
> Energy efficiency potential in Dubai: between ^{5} _____ and _____ hours of sunshine a day all year round.
>
> Solar park at Seih Al Dahal: energy generating capacity of ^{7} _____ million kilowatt hours per year. It will soon provide ^{8} _____% of the city's energy needs, rising to ^{9} _____% by 2030. By this time, the solar park will cover ^{10} _____ km^2 of desert.

LANGUAGE DEVELOPMENT (15 marks)

4 Use the definitions and sentences to complete the puzzle. 1 mark for each correct answer.

1↓

2→	C	H	A	L	L	E	N	G	E
3→				P			E		
4→				F			N		
5→		M					E		
6→			R				R		
7→				D			A		
8→	C						T		
9→			C				I		
10→					V		O		
11→				M			N		

1 The act of producing electricity.
2 A difficult situation or problem.
3 If somebody or something has a lot of _____, they may be very successful in the future.
4 The purpose of something – what it is designed to do.
5 The act of looking after something (e.g. a machine) so that it keeps working.
6 A large man-made body of water, often behind a dam.
7 Another name for a disadvantage or problem with something.
8 The act of using something – the opposite of production.
9 The total amount that something can produce or hold.
10 The space that something takes up.
11 The part of a country or continent which is not an island.

5 Choose the correct option (a-d) to complete the sentences. 1 mark for each correct answer.

1 Solar power is still not capable of generating large amounts of electricity. _____, most energy companies believe it will be important in the near future.
   a Therefore b Nevertheless c What's more d In addition

2 Coal and oil are very harmful to the environment, _____ we need to invest in alternative sources of energy.
   a so b in addition c moreover d on the other hand

3 Nuclear power is a good source of cheap electricity. _____, it can be extremely dangerous when there is an accident.
   a Therefore b So c As a result d On the other hand

4 We want to use less electricity in our office. _____, we would like you to switch off the lights when you leave a room.
   a In addition b Therefore c Moreover d Nevertheless

5 Wind power can be one of the cheapest sources of renewable energy. _____, it is not at all harmful to the environment.
   a Therefore b On the other hand c Furthermore d As a result

TOTAL ___ / 35

Name: .... **Date:** ....

LISTENING (20 marks)

LISTENING 1

1 (🔊 9.1) Listen to a radio programme about an art exhibition. Write H (host), C (critic), V (visitor) or A (artist) next to the opinion. 1 mark for each correct answer.

1 The paintings show the strong emotions of the artist. _____

2 The pictures look like they were done by a small child. _____

3 I don't want to tell you what the pictures show. _____

4 I like pictures to look realistic. _____

5 I prefer the countryside to the city. _____

6 The green colours might represent fields and hills. _____

7 Everybody takes different stories from the pictures. _____

8 I feel relaxed when I look at the pictures. _____

9 The shapes remind me of an animal and water. _____

10 Feelings are more important than understanding what a picture shows. _____

LISTENING 2

2 (🔊 9.2) Listen to an informal debate about design. Tick the points mentioned in the discussion. 2 marks for each correct answer.

1 The furniture in the reception area does not create the right impression. _____

2 The design of the furniture in the photographs is very modern. _____

3 The existing furniture is not very comfortable. _____

4 The furniture in the pictures comes from an art gallery. _____

5 Furniture can help patients to believe the medical centre is good. _____

6 The medical centre has a problem with the quality of its doctors. _____

7 Many patients have complained that the reception area is dirty. _____

8 It is necessary to replace the furniture with something newer. _____

9 Colour is an essential part of good design. _____

10 The chairs in the photographs don't look very comfortable. _____

LANGUAGE DEVELOPMENT (15 marks)

3 Replace the words in bold with the correct form of a word or phrase from the box. 1 mark for each correct answer.

appreciate   comment   ~~demonstrate~~   focus   inspiration   interpret   junction   reject   remove
restore   self-expression

1   Through his sculptures, he has **shown** that he is a very talented artist.   _demonstrated_

2   I offered to pay $1000 for the painting, but she **said no to** my offer. _____

3   You may think street art is very creative, but if it's illegal, it needs to be **taken away**. _____

4   Most people don't **understand and value** the importance of design. _____

5   Many people have tried to **understand and explain** her paintings. _____

6   The art gallery is near a **place where two or more roads meet**. _____

7   I think all children should paint – it's a wonderful form of **showing who you really are**. _____

8   I get my **ideas and motivation** from the natural world. _____

9   He works in a museum, where he **fixes** damaged paintings. _____

10   Many people have **given an opinion** on the originality of his work. _____

11   I don't think you need to understand art – you should **concentrate your attention** on how it makes you feel. _____

4 Complete the text with the words in the box. 1 mark for each correct answer.

granted   actually   reality   as   matter

Many people think that design is something that belongs in galleries, but in [1]_____ good design is everywhere. We take it for [2]_____that the things we buy will look good, but the fact of the [3]_____is that they only look good because they have been carefully designed. It may seem [4]_____if design is less important than whether something works or not, but [5]_____, without good design, nobody would buy a product, no matter how well it works.

TOTAL ___ / 35

REVIEW TEST 10

Name: .... **Date:** ....

LISTENING (20 marks)

LISTENING 1

1 (◀) **10.1** Listen to a discussion on midlife crises between two students, Mike and Sonia. Complete the notes with one or two words. 1 mark for each correct answer.

Midlife crises:
- Professor Philips (age: about ¹_____) has just bought a
  ²_____.
- When people have a mid life crisis, they realize they are getting older and decide to make big life ³_____. Many people in their 50s suddenly have spare ⁴_____ and money. They don't have to look after ⁵_____ and it's their first chance to have ⁶_____ in a long time.
- Mike's uncle (age: nearly ⁷_____ has just bought an ⁸_____ _____.
- In a mid life crisis, people worry they have spent too much of their life doing ordinary things and decide to do meaningful things like travel around the ⁹_____.
- Sonia's mother is writing a ¹⁰_____.

LISTENING 2

2 (◀) **10.2** Listen to a student's presentation about life expectancy in Russia. Complete the table. 1 mark for each correct answer.

	1950s	1986	1994	1998	2003	2011
Men	60					
Women	67					

LANGUAGE DEVELOPMENT (15 marks)

3 Match the sentence halves. 1 mark for each correct answer.

1 If you save money for your retirement   a   it is expensive and you don't really need it.

2 Your assets are   b   people who you are responsible for, e.g. your children.

3 Your ancestors are   c   you can spend it when you're older.

4 If something is described as a luxury   d   all your family members who lived before you.

5 Your dependants are   e   all the things you own.

4 Complete the table with the correct formal verb from the box. 1 mark for each correct answer.

contribute   assist   indicate   participate
devote

informal / neutral verb	formal verb
give oneself to something	1_____ oneself to something
give something	2_____ something
take part in something	3_____ in something
help somebody	4_____ somebody
show something	5_____ something

5 Choose the correct expressions (a–d) to complete the sentences. 1 mark for each correct answer.

1 My neighbour has _____ to let me park my car in his drive.

   a allowed   b consented   c persuaded   d threatened

2 I don't know where they are – they _____ to tell us where they were going.

   a refused   b caused   c arranged   d advised

3 My grandmother is really happy with her new wheelchair. It has _____ her to go out much more.

   a offered   b consented   c allowed   d entitled

4 My grandfather _____ me to start my own business.

   a offered   b advised   c consented   d managed

5 I don't _____ to live in a care home when I'm old. I'd prefer to live with my family.

   a cause   b entitle   c allow   d want

TOTAL ___ / 35

ADDITIONAL SPEAKING TASK 1

You are going to give a two-minute presentation on the following question:

When we buy petrol for our cars, where does the money go?

1 Look at the pie chart. It shows a percentage breakdown of the price of petrol in a European country. Think about possible causes and effects of the different figures in the chart.

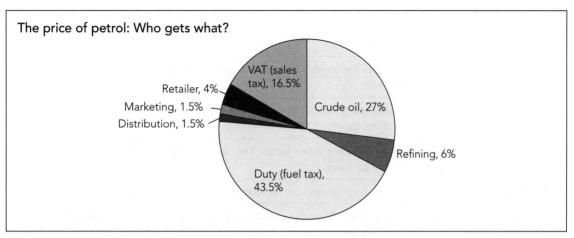

The price of petrol: Who gets what?

VAT (sales tax), 16.5%
Retailer, 4%
Marketing, 1.5%
Distribution, 1.5%
Crude oil, 27%
Refining, 6%
Duty (fuel tax), 43.5%

2 Work alone to prepare your presentation. Put the most important points in your presentation first and support them with data. Write notes and a conclusion to help you organize your presentation.

3 Work with a partner. Give your presentation.

MODEL LANGUAGE

PRESENTING DATA IN A PIE CHART

Cause–effect relationships

Due to …

… because of …

As a result [of this],

Consequently, …

… which therefore …

Describing charts and data

I'd like to talk about …

There has been a lot of discussion in the media recently about …

Many people believe that …

However, others have pointed out that …

However, I would like to show that …

Let's look at some data.

If you consider the information in this chart …

Describing a pie chart

The largest part of the cost is …, at X%.

That's more than half the cost.

… accounts for X% of the cost.

… and … each make up about X% of the cost, or a total of X% …

Three parts are related to …

Together, they make up X% of the price.

Drawing conclusions from data

This pie chart shows …

Firstly … / Secondly … / Next, I'd like to draw your attention to …

You'll notice that …

As you can see …

This data shows that …

This means that it may be possible to …

Finally, the chart shows …

Looking at the chart, we can conclude that …

In summary, the data shows that …

ADDITIONAL SPEAKING TASK 2

You are going to participate in a group discussion on the following question:

What is the best course for someone who wants to be an astronaut?

1 Work alone. Arturo wants to become an astronaut. He has chosen five possible university courses to study. Read the notes and give each course a mark out of 10 for how useful you think it will be for becoming an astronaut.

Courses for becoming an astronaut

Mechanical and electrical engineering	Useful for understanding how a spacecraft works, and fixing broken machines _____
International relations	Because space travel involves people from many different countries; useful for learning other languages. _____
Biology	Useful for doing experiments and understanding how people's bodies function in space. _____
Astrophysics	Gives a deep theoretical understanding of how space works. _____
Maths	To show that I'm really intelligent; also good for gaining experience of working with computers. _____

2 Work in a group. Discuss the usefulness of each course in turn. Be ready to disagree with other people's opinioins. Try to reach an agreement on the best course for Arturo.

MODEL LANGUAGE

PARTICIAPTING IN A DISCUSSION

Stating preferences with would

I'd rather … / Would you rather …?

I'd like to …

I'd prefer it if you … / Would you prefer … or …?

Giving an opinion and making suggestions

The most important factor is probably …

I think the least important thing is …

Why don't we …?

What if we say that … is the most important factor?

Have you considered taking … into account?

I feel it's important to really focus on …

Agreeing

I couldn't agree more.

I'm with you on that point.

That's a valid argument.

Respectfully disagreeing

I can see what you're saying, but I have a different opinion.

I'm not sure I share that viewpoint.

I'm sorry, but I have to disagree.

Yes, but have you considered the other factors involved?

Compromizing and finalizing a decision

I see. That's understandable.

OK, I see your point. / OK, I think we all can live with that.

You might be right about that.

Right. We've made a decision. / Right. I think we've come to an agreement.

ADDITIONAL SPEAKING TASK 3

You are going to take part in a debate on the following statement:

Governments should force people to lead healthier lives.

1 Work in two groups.

Group A: You work for a pharmaceutical company. You agree with the above statement.

Group B: You work for a human rights organisation. You disagree with the above statement.

2 In your groups, prepare and practise an opening statement for the debate. Think about your opponents' views and make notes about what they might say in response to your statement.

3 Have the debate. After the debate, discuss the way the arguments were presented and try to agree which group won the debate.

MODEL LANGUAGE

TAKING PART IN A DEBATE

Asking challenging questions

Let me ask you this. Can you prove that …?

If …, why aren't we using/doing it?

Giving information to support your position

It may not sound like a lot, but, this is actually …

There isn't one single scientific study that proves that …

In my country, … . This system works very well.

Addressing the other person's argument

Clearly [name of other speaker] and I agree that …

You're absolutely right that …, but …?

I'd definitely like to challenge the idea that …

I disagree with [name of other speaker] on that point.

So while you're right, that doesn't mean …

If …, that doesn't logically mean …

Well, I'm sure [name of other speaker] is a very good [doctor], but I think …

Using specific persuasive language

Obviously, …

Supposing …?

How would you feel if …?

We can clearly see that …

It's obvious that if you want to have …, you need to …

The most important thing to remember is that …

ADDITIONAL SPEAKING TASK 4

You are going to complete a risk assessment and try to think of ways to reduce the risks of the incidents in the following table occurring:

annual incidents report (accident, illness or injury): jungle adventure tours		
incident	total number of cases	% of total number of incidents
1 insect bites	34	19%
2 snake bites	5	2%
3 heatstroke	31	17%
4 minor cuts	44	24%
5 slipping/tripping and falling	67	37%
total number of incidents	181	100%
total visitors last year	754	

1 Work in small groups. Analyse the statistics in the table. For each type of incident, discuss the risk level (from very low to very high) and try to think of ways to reduce the risks of each incident occurring.

2 Report back to the class. Did each group have similar ideas about how to reduce the risks of the incidents occurring? Why / Why not?

MODEL LANGUAGE

DISCUSSING STATISTICS AND PROBABILITY

Talking about statistical evidence

We calculate only X% of visitors had …

Or putting it another way, X visitors …

By far the most common issue was … .

After that, the next most common issue was …, with X cases.

That's X visitors, or X% of all medical issues.

Fortunately, … and … were the least common. Together they made up X% of the issues we treated.

Language for clarification

What I mean is …

I'm talking about …

In other words, …

By 'X', I mean … / When I say 'X', I'm thinking of …

Expressions for talking about likelihood and probability

one hundred percent certain

highly probable

definitely possible

extremely unlikely

absolutely impossible

ADDITIONAL SPEAKING TASK 5

You are going to explain a process to a partner.

Choose an object that you know well that contains several parts, e.g. a mobile phone, a bicycle, a chair, etc. Describe the process of recycling it.

1 Work alone. Draw a dependency diagram for recycling your object. There should be at least six stages. If you don't know how to recycle it, use your imagination, or ask your teacher for help with vocabulary.

2 Describe your recycling process to a partner. While you are listening you should make notes on the process your partner is describing.

3 Describe your recycling processes back to each other. Did you get your partner's process right? If not, what was different?

MODEL LANGUAGE

DESCRIBING A PROCESS

Signposting

Our topic is … and I'll divide the lecture into X parts.

The first part of the talk will look at …

We've looked at …, but are there any …?

Let's turn now to the … process.

In short, …

First steps

Firstly, … / First of all, … / To begin with, … / The process starts with … / Initially, …

Next steps

After … / Then … / Next, … / Subsequently, … / The next step … / After that, … / Afterwards, … / Later, …

Things that happen at the same time

Simultaneously, … / Meanwhile, … / … at the same time

Results and consequences

Consequently, … / … so … / As a result, …

Final steps

Last of all, … / Finally, …

ADDITIONAL SPEAKING TASK 6

You are going to give a problem and solution presentation on the following topic.

The Antarctic environment

Antarctica

Antarctic Continent: Approximately 3,661,000 km^2. 1/12 of the world's entire land area. Contains 90% of the world's ice (about 70% of the world's fresh water).

Treaties:

- Antarctic Treaty (1959): International community agreed to work to maintain and protect region and co-operate on scientific research
- Madrid Protocol (1991): Confirmed Antarctica as an area devoted to world peace and science. Prohibited exploitation of area's natural resources (coal, natural gas, etc.)

Wildlife:

- Plants: mainly small plants and mosses
- Land animals: mostly microscopic creatures (mites, lice, etc.)
- Marine animals: penguins, blue whales, killer whales, seals, fish etc.

Current examples of human impact in Antarctic:

- Melting ice and other changes caused by global warming
- Over-fishing in Antarctic area

Earlier examples of human impact in Antarctic, now prohibited under Madrid Treaty:

- Hunting animals for economic benefit
- Killing and disturbing endangered species
- Soil contamination as a result of mining
- Sea pollution and waste materials from ships

---

1 Work in groups to plan a presentation. Use the model language to help you.

2 Work different groups to give your presentation. Were the presentations in your group similar? Why/why not?

....

MODEL LANGUAGE

GIVING A PROBLEM AND SOLUTION PRESENTATION

Giving background information

The UN reports that …

The UN gives the example of …

According to the UN, …

Data shows that …

Explaining a problem

The problem is that …

The two main problems are … and …

Signposting

The subject of my talk today is … / Today I'm going to talk about …

I have three main points to make in this talk … / Let's begin by looking at …

Let's turn now to … / Moving on now to …

But, what does this mean for …? / Let's consider this in more detail …

To put it another way, … / So what I'm saying is …

A good example of this is … / To give you an example …

That's all I have to say on that point. / That concludes this part of the talk …

To summarize, … / I'd like to now recap …

ADDITIONAL SPEAKING TASK 7

You are going to discuss a problem and possible solution for the following topic in a group.

A university plans to open a new languages department as soon as possible. The department needs four lecture halls, each for 100+ people, at least ten classrooms with room for up to 20 people and other facilities to make it attractive to students. It has €1.4 million to spend on the building.

1 Work in two pairs. One pair are the project developers. The second pair are university representatives. In your pairs, look at the problem and the proposed solution.

> **Proposed solution:**
> Build a new building on the outskirts of the city, 20km from the rest of the university. The cost would be around €1.6 million for a building with six large lecture halls and fifteen classrooms, plus a sports room, library and social rooms. The building could be ready in two years.
>
> **Project developers:** You will present the positive aspects of your solution to the university representatives. What problems might the client identify with your solution? How could you respond?
>
> **University representatives:** You will listen to a presentation from the project developers. Ask questions about any information they don't mention in their solution, or anything you aren't sure about. What problems can you identify in their solution?

2 Discuss the problem and solution as a group. Could you come to an agreement about what to do?

MODEL LANGUAGE

DISCUSSING PROBLEMS AND SOLUTIONS

Presenting a problem

The problem is …

The main issue is …

We need to find a way around …

Making suggestions

Could we …?

Should we consider …?

Have you thought about …?

Why don't we …?

We could consider using …

How about if we …?

Can / Could I suggest we …?

Wouldn't it be better if …?

What about …?

This would probably be better with …

I strongly recommend that we …

I feel confident we can …

Responding to suggested solutions

I like your thinking. I agree completely.

I think that's a great idea.

Let's do it.

That's a great idea, but I'm not sure it addresses the problem.

We thought that might be an option at first, but now we realize it won't work.

That seems an obvious solution, but it doesn't address the issue of …

You've described …, but actually, that's …

As it stands, this plan would be very controversial.

… is a great idea, but in my view the only viable option is to use …

ADDITIONAL SPEAKING TASK 8

You are going to participate in a chaired discussion on the following topic:

How can we make our city/country energy independent?

1 Work in groups of three or four. Look at the agenda. Each student will be chair for one numbered item on the agenda.

> **Agenda**
> 1 Current level of energy consumption
> 2 Possible sources of producing energy
> 3 Ways of reducing consumption
> 4 Summary and conclusions

2 Work alone to plan what to say for your agenda point. Think of two or three ideas to raise and make notes on the language you might use.

3 Have the discussion. Make sure you keep your part of the discussion on topic. Did you come to any conclusions at the end of the discussion? Why / Why not?

MODEL LANGUAGE

PARTICIPATING IN A CHAIRED DISCUSSION

Persuasive techniques

Why don't we consider …?

Have you thought more about my idea of …?

There are other considerations. We'd have to look at …, for example.

On that point, we could …

The fact is, …

I see what you mean, but have you considered the fact that …?

I can assure you that the company wouldn't …

I don't think we need to worry about …

I can't help but feel that … would be too ambitious.

I'm not convinced that …

Asking for input, summarizing and keeping a discussion moving

Does anyone have anything to say about this idea?

What are your views on the proposal?

I'd just like to recap the key points so far.

So, to sum up so far …

Sorry, but that's not really what we're discussing right now.

Sorry, but could you hold that thought until I've finished, please?

Being firm but polite

Sorry, but … / Could you possibly …? / Would you mind …?

Thank you for pointing that out, but it isn't really what we're talking about.

Please could you save that for later in the discussion?

ADDITIONAL SPEAKING TASK 9

You are going to participate in an informal debate on the following topic:

Some of the senior staff at your university/college would like to stage a high profile art exhibition. They are deciding on whether to go ahead with the exhibition, as there is some opposition to it.

1 Work in groups of three students. Decide if your group is for or against holding the exhibition, and why. Think of two statements to use in the debate, then predict how other speakers might respond to your statements. Practise your presentation as a group.

2 Work with two people from different groups. Have the debate. Could you come to any decisions or make any next steps in your debate?

MODEL LANGUAGE

PARTICIAPTING IN AN INFORMAL DEBATE

Debate statements, responses and decisions

I (don't) think we should …

You could say that, but I think …

Let's put together a proposal.

Let's look further at …

Expressing contrasting opinions

At first glance, it looks as if … / Many people think that … / It looks like …

We take it for granted that … / Some people say …

It may seem like … / It seems as if …

… but in fact, … / However, actually, … / In reality, … / The truth/fact of the matter is …

Hedging

Personally, I'm not really sure … / I'm not an expert, but … / All I know is … / For me, …

You could say that, however actually … / That's true in part, but I think … /

You may be right, but I wonder if … / I see what you're saying, but maybe …

Restating somebody's point

Do you mean …?

So what you're saying is …

In other words, you don't think …

So, if I understand you correctly, …?

You are going to give a presentation to a seminar group on the following topic:

Give a presentation on employment levels for people in Country A over 60 and the impact this is likely to have on its society in the future.

1 Work in groups. Look at the graph showing the employment statistics for the over 60s in a small country between 1950 and 2050. All numbers are in thousands. Choose one line on the graph (A, B, C or D) to describe.

FACT FILE

Life expectancy rose from 59 in 1950 to 75 in 2010 as a result of continuing health improvements.

In 1997, the official retirement age rose from 64 to 67, followed by another rise to 70 in the mid-2020s.

The population of the whole country grew dramatically in the 20th century, but has stabilized and is now falling slowly.

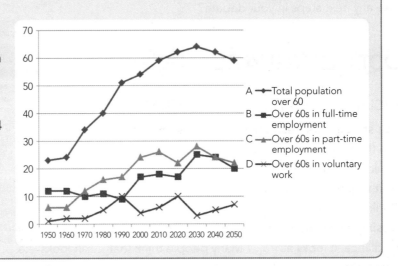

A — Total population over 60
B — Over 60s in full-time employment
C — Over 60s in part-time employment
D — Over 60s in voluntary work

2 Write notes on the following areas: Presenting your data; Talking about the causes and effects of your data; Comparing your data to that of the other lines on the graph. Practise your presentation in your group.

3 Form a new group with people who have looked at the other lines on the graph. Perform your presentation to your new group. Were your presentations similar? Why / Why not?

MODEL LANGUAGE

PRESENTING DATA IN A LINE GRAPH

Referencing data in a presentation

As you can see in the graph, between [year] and [year], … will shoot up from [number] to [number].

If you look at the graph, we can see … peaks at [number] in [year].

Between [year] and [year], … is due to plummet from [number] to [number].

If you look at the data provided, you can see … remains steady from [year] to [year].

After peaking in [year], … will fluctuate and then stabilize at about [number].

After a steady increase in population between [year] and [year], the population is due to fall slowly.

Explaining causes and effects

The steady increase in … between [year] and [year] was the result of …

The sharp rise in … between [year] and [year] was brought about by …

The predicted decrease in … from [year] onwards can be traced back to …

The number of … will increase steeply after [year] owing to …

… between [year] and the present account for …

ACKNOWLEDGEMENTS

Author acknowledgements

Many thanks to my editor, Ruth Cox, for all her support, guidance and encouragement. Thanks also to Barry Tadman for managing the project so effectively and professionally.

Jeremy Day

Publisher acknowledgements

The publishers are extremely grateful to the following people and their students for reviewing and trialling this course during its development. The course has benefited hugely from your insightful comments and feedback.

Mr M.K. Adjibade, King Saud University, Saudi Arabia; Canan Aktug, Bursa Technical University, Turkey; Olwyn Alexander, Heriot Watt University, UK; Valerie Anisy, Damman University, Saudi Arabia; Anwar Al-Fetlawi, University of Sharjah, UAE; Laila Al-Qadhi, Kuwait University, Kuwait; Tahani Al-Taha, University of Dubai, UAE; Ozlem Atalay, Middle East Technical University, Turkey; Seda Merter Ataygul, Bursa Technical University Turkey; Harika Altug, Bogazici University, Turkey; Kwab Asare, University of Westminster, UK; Erdogan Bada, Cukurova University, Turkey; Cem Balcikanli, Gazi University, Turkey; Gaye Bayri, Anadolu University, Turkey; Meher Ben Lakhdar, Sohar University, Oman; Emma Biss, Girne American University, UK; Dogan Bulut, Meliksah University, Turkey; Sinem Bur, TED University, Turkey; Alison Chisholm, University of Sussex, UK; Dr. Panidnad Chulerk , Rangsit University, Thailand; Sedat Cilingir, Bilgi University, Istanbul, Turkey; Sarah Clark, Nottingham Trent International College, UK; Elaine Cockerham, Higher College of Technology, Muscat, Oman; Asli Derin, Bilgi University, Turkey; Steven Douglass, University of Sunderland, UK; Jacqueline Einer, Sabanci University, Turkey; Basak Erel, Anadolu University, Turkey; Hande Lena Erol, Piri Reis Maritime University, Turkey; Gulseren Eyuboglu, Ozyegin University, Turkey; Dr. Majid Gharawi and colleagues at the English Language Centre, Jazan University, Saudi Arabia; Muge Gencer, Kemerburgaz University, Turkey; Jeff Gibbons, King Fahed University of Petroleum and Minerals, Saudi Arabia; Maxine Gilway, Bristol University, UK; Dr Christina Gitsaki, HCT, Dubai Men's College, UAE; Sam Fenwick, Sohar University, Oman; Peter Frey, International House, Doha, Qatar; Neil Harris, Swansea University, UK; Vicki Hayden, College of the North Atlantic, Qatar; Ajarn Naratip Sharp Jindapitak, Prince of Songkla University, Hatyai, Thailand; Joud Jabri-Pickett, United Arab Emirates University, Al Ain, UAE; Aysel Kilic, Anadolu University, Turkey; Ali Kimav, Anadolu University, Turkey; Bahar Kiziltunali, Izmir University of Economics, Turkey; Kamil Koc, Ozel Kasimoglu Coskun Lisesi, Turkey; Ipek Korman-Tezcan, Yeditepe University, Turkey; Philip Lodge, Dubai Men's College, UAE; Iain Mackie, Al Rowdah University, Abu Dhabi, UAE; Katherine Mansfield, University of Westminster, UK; Kassim Mastan, King Saud University, Saudi Arabia; Elspeth McConnell, Newham College, UK; Lauriel Mehdi, American University of Sharjah, UAE; Dorando Mirkin-Dick, Bell International Institute, UK; Dr Sita Musigrungsi, Prince of Songkla University, Hatyai, Thailand; Mark Neville, Al Hosn University, Abu Dhabi, UAE; Shirley Norton, London School of English, UK; James Openshaw, British Study Centres, UK; Hale Ottolini, Mugla Sitki Kocman University, Turkey; David Palmer, University of Dubai, UAE; Michael Pazinas, United Arab Emirates University, UAE; Troy Priest, Zayed University, UAE; Alison Ramage Patterson, Jeddah, Saudi Arabia; Paul Rogers, Qatar Skills Academy, Qatar; Josh Round, Saint George International, UK; Harika Saglicak, Bogazici University, Turkey; Asli Saracoglu, Isik University, Turkey; Neil Sarkar, Ealing, Hammersmith and West London College, UK; Nancy Shepherd, Bahrain University, Bahrain; Jonathan Smith, Sabanci University, Turkey; Peter Smith, United Arab Emirates University, UAE; Adem Soruc, Fatih University Istanbul, Turkey; Dr Peter Stanfield, HCT, Madinat Zayed & Ruwais Colleges, UAE; Maria Agata Szczerbik, United Arab Emirates University, Al Ain, UAE; Burcu Tezcan-Unal, Bilgi University, Turkey; Dr Nakonthep Tipayasuparat, Rangsit University, Thailand; Scott Thornbury, The New School, New York, USA; Susan Toth, HCT, Dubai Men's Campus, Dubai, UAE; Melin Unal, Ege University, Izmir, Turkey; Aylin Unaldi, Bogaziçi University, Turkey; Colleen Wackrow, Princess Nourah bint Abdulrahman University, Riyadh, Saudi Arabia; Gordon Watts, Study Group, Brighton UK; Po Leng Wendelkin, INTO at University of East Anglia, UK; Halime Yildiz, Bilkent University, Ankara, Turkey; Ferhat Yilmaz, Kahramanmaras Sutcu Imam University, Turkey.

Special thanks to Peter Lucantoni for sharing his expertise, both pedagogical and cultural.

Special thanks also to Michael Pazinas for writing the *Research projects* which feature at the end of every unit. Michael has first-hand experience of teaching in and developing materials for the paperless classroom. He has worked in Greece, the Middle East and the UK. Prior to his current position as Curriculum and Assessment Coordinator for the Foundation Program at the United Arab Emirates University he was an English teacher for the British Council, the University of Exeter and several private language institutes. Michael is also a graphic designer, involved in instructional design and educational eBook development. He is an advocate of challenge-based language learning.

Photo acknowledgements

p.8: (1) © Eric Limon/Shutterstock; p.8: (2) © szefai/Shutterstock; p.8: (3) © Steven Vidler/Eurasia Press/Corbis. All videos stills by kind permission of © Discovery Communications LLC 2014

Dictionary

Cambridge dictionaries are the world's most widely used dictionaries for learners of English. Available at three levels (Cambridge Essential English Dictionary, Cambridge Learner's Dictionary and Cambridge Advanced Learner's Dictionary),

they provide easy-to-understand definitions, example sentences, and help in avoiding typical mistakes. The dictionaries are also available online at dictionary.cambridge.org. © Cambridge University Press, reproduced with permission.

Corpus

Development of this publication has made use of the Cambridge English Corpus (CEC). The CEC is a multi-billion word computer database of contemporary spoken and written English. It includes British English, American English and other varieties of English. It also includes the Cambridge Learner Corpus, developed in collaboration with Cambridge English Language Assessment. Cambridge University Press has built up the CEC to provide evidence about language use that helps to produce better language teaching materials.

Typeset by Integra